STOP ARGUING
AND START UNDERSTANDING

Stop Arguing and Start Understanding

EIGHT STEPS TO SOLVING FAMILY CONFLICTS

David C. Hall, M.D.

MONTLAKE FAMILY PRESS

The following publishers have generously given permission to use extended quotations from copyrighted works. From *There's a Hole in My Sidewalk: The Romance of Self-Discovery,* by Portia Nelson. Copyright 1994 by Portia Nelson. Reprinted by permission of Beyond Words Publishing. From *Getting Past No* by William Ury, copyright ©1991. Used by permission of Bantam Books, a division of Random House, Inc.

Montlake Family Press
2200 - 24th Ave. East, Seattle, WA 98112
Phone/Fax: 888-565-3404   www.FamilyHealing.com

Individual Sales. This book is available through most bookstores or can be ordered directly from Montlake Family Press at the address above.

Quantity Sales. Special discounts are available on quantity purchases by corporations, associations, and others. For details, contact the "Special Sales Department" at the address above.

Printed in the United States of America

Library of Congress Cataloging-in-Publication Data

Hall, David C., 1946-
    Stop arguing and start understanding : eight steps to
solving family conflicts / David C. Hall. —lst cd.
    p. cm.
    Includes bibliographical references and index.
    ISBN 0-9710500-0-7
    1. Parenting—Psychological aspects.   2. Parent and
child. I. Title
HQ755.8.H35 2001   649'.1
                        QB101-700693

Disclaimer: This book is not intended for use in the treatment or prevention of disease or as a substitute for medical treatment or as an alternative to medical advice. All matters regarding your health require medical supervision. Please consult your physician or health professional about any condition that may require diagnosis or medical attention.

Every attempt has been made to present accurate and timely information. We have used many sources, including our own professional and personal experiences, to compile the information found in this guide. The medical field is constantly changing, which will account for many of the changes in references, resources, information, statistics, technology, approaches, or techniques that no doubt will occur by the time this book is purchased or read. Many individuals, scientists, and medical, legal, and healthcare professionals may voice their own findings and opinions, which may differ significantly from those included in this guide. Therefore, nothing contained herein should constitute an absolute with regard to this subject matter or be considered a substitute for legal, medical, or psychological advice.

The author and publisher assume neither liability nor responsibility to any person or entity with respect to any direct or indirect loss or damage caused, or alleged to be caused, by the information contained herein, or for errors, omissions, inaccuracies, or any other inconsistency within these pages, or for unintentional slights against people or organizations. The author and publisher are not associated with any manufacturers of the products mentioned and are not guaranteeing the safety of these products.

Editorial Services: PeopleSpeak
Indexing: Rachel Rice
Composition: Beverly Butterfield, Girl of the West Productions; Kristina Kachele

FIRST EDITION
05 04 03 02 01 00   10 9 8 7 6 5 4 3 2 1

To my parents, whose lifelong gifts of love and respect
will always be their most precious legacies to me,

and

To two incomparable apostles for healthy families:

Eyad El Sarraj, M.D., and
Michael B. Rothenberg, M.D.

May your legacies inspire others as
they have inspired me.

CONTENTS

STEP 6

FIND FRIENDS FOR YOURSELF AND YOUR FAMILY 193

STEP 7

PURSUE SPIRITUAL HEALTH 215

STEP 8

REFUSE TO GIVE UP 229

ACKNOWLEDGMENTS

INSPIRATION AND SUPPORT through the many years of writing this book came from family, friends, colleagues, and patients. They have made me a blessed person in an abundant world.

My own rich family experience underlies every word—generous and devoted parents, three sisters who have always cherished me, a wife who is a prophetic soul mate, two thoroughly satisfying grown sons, and wonderful daughters-in-law.

I thank God for a robust faith that love and generosity can reverse the travesties of indifference and hatred and hold us safely in community with each other and our precious Earth.

For two decades my patients and I have battled their legacies of violence and mental disorders. We work together steadfastly to reclaim their right to live with hope, respect, kindness, and peace.

I am grateful to the special people who waded through various drafts of this book. They added their wisdom, inspiration, friendship, and love—Paul Herstein, Roy and Leigh Farrell, Jon Hall, Judy Lipton, Cindy Russell, Deborah Hall, and Anne Hall. Sharon Goldinger and her colleagues at PeopleSpeak gave invaluable guidance in organizing my passion for helping troubled families and helping me to write a better book.

My heartfelt thank-you to each of you.

FOREWORD

DEALING WITH FAMILIES in conflict is like passing through a jungle. There are no clear paths. Each step must be taken with caution; fear and danger lurk in every shadow. Most who have been hurt as children do not want to re-enter the "jungle" of their past.

Dr. Albert Schweitzer left his lucrative European medical practice to work in the African jungles. He found the jungle to be a place of great healing. Dr. David Hall, a graduate of Harvard College and the University of Washington Medical School, could easily have had a lucrative and comfortable practice anywhere he chose. He chose instead to work with the most difficult cases where there was the least hope. He has worked with victims of serious child abuse and neglect for decades. There are no quick fixes or miracle drugs for these cases.

Few clinicians have the skill and compassion to help their clients dig deep enough to truly heal such wounds. David Hall is one of them. The tools he has found for healing the deepest emotional injuries are very effective for other family problems as well.

David Hall's book is important for what it is as well as for what it is not. It will not mislead you with trendy labels or quick fixes that, like plastic wrap, cover problems but do very little to heal them.

This book does not trumpet any shortcuts where altering one part of your life will somehow fix the rest. It also does not make problems so technical that nothing can be done without therapy. It takes the more difficult path of addressing you as a whole person with a unique perspective.

Few clinicians are sufficiently skilled to help family members recover from the worst of injuries. Fewer still are those who can distill what they do and write about it in an accessible manner.

David Hall has done this and more: he provides a set of tools born of twenty years of medical practice that extends far beyond psychiatry. Many books push beleaguered parents to buy into new techniques when the parents barely have enough energy to keep going. This book does just the opposite: it empowers first by bringing greater tenacity and compassion to what you are doing before considering different ways of parenting. The gentle wisdom flowing through these chapters makes rereading just as beneficial as the first reading.

In both layout and content, this book is a wise friend—a friend who listens without lecturing, who supports without judgment, and who honors your commitment to parenting.

Good books on parenting help you see your problems in a new way. Great books help you see yourself in a new way. Dr. Albert Schweitzer wrote, "You will never find true happiness until you determine how it is you are to serve." David Hall has been serving parents and families for over thirty years. His work helps us each find our unique path through the jungle of doubt and frustration into the happiness of knowing that we truly served our children, our communities, and ourselves.

JOHN KYDD, MSW, JD
Past President
Association of Family and Conciliation Courts

INTRODUCTION

MANY FAMILIES HOLD a world of hurt.

Currently in the United States nearly half of all children go through the divorce of their parents. Nearly half of all adults experience disabling emotional distress sometime in their lives. More than a million children are referred to the police or child protection agencies for abuse or neglect each year—and many more cases are never reported. Suicide, according to the U.S. surgeon general, is at epidemic proportions.[1]

At the same time, television, movies, video games, news media, and popular music saturate our children and us with oversexed and violent images while minimizing how disturbing these images can be. Advertising is everywhere, telling us we need to drink more beer, buy fancier cars, wear designer clothes, and look more like anorectic or steroid-pumped models. Parenting in this environment can easily become overwhelming, and so can the search for answers.

I have spent many years helping families find the answers they're looking for. My first inspiration for helping troubled families came from Leo and his friends, who lived in the dingy, gray-and-brown world of a 1930s housing project in Cambridge, Massachusetts. Leo was a seven-year-old plugger and I was a freshman at Harvard College. He and his friends wanted companionship, something fun to do, and someone to take an interest in them. I wanted to feel less homesick for my family in Seattle, Washington. So two of us from Harvard and eight boys from the Roosevelt Towers gathered every week in a wire-windowed basement to talk, play games, plan field trips, and learn to get along with each other. Leo always seemed amazed to be with us. He and the other boys became the highlight of my week and a surrogate family. Many times I tried to imagine my life had I been raised as they were.

For two of the next three years I worked in similar programs with children and teenagers from other Boston area housing projects. The hope I saw in their eyes still inspires me. Their fear and aloneness has stayed with me. I later finished medical school and became a psychiatrist to children and adults in emotional turmoil. With this book I hope to reach out again to families in pain with an offering of inspiration, information, and ideas for change.

This book offers many practical suggestions you can use right away to change your family. It also has many moments of reflection. Most of these reflections are based on my experiences with my patients and my professional knowledge; some are spiritual in nature. I want you to believe as strongly as I do that life is precious and the human spirit can cope with almost anything and that you can change the painful patterns in your family.

Stop Arguing and Start Understanding is only the start of your family's journey to health. It will help you change the way you think about your family's problems, show you where you can find the help and strength you need, and inspire you to keep going for as long as it takes to make your family safe and loving.

You already have all the energy you need to heal your family. (If you are so depressed that you don't have energy for anything at all, see page 47.) In the pages that follow, you will learn to save your energy for actions that create hope and success rather than wasting your energy on dead-end arguments and other contests of will. If you are a thoughtful and determined person who wants to mend your family's hurtful ways, you can do it with a workable plan and the tenacity to see it through. That's what this book is all about.

My approach to family healing is built on six principles:

• Every person is precious and deserves a healthy family.
• Anyone can change for the better.
• One determined parent can make a world of difference.
• Good information gives us better choices.
• Life gets better as we learn to work together.
• What helps us grow spiritually helps our families find fulfillment and peace.

Fortunately, families don't get into serious trouble every time something goes wrong. We get into serious trouble when we can't break the habit of hurting each other.

There are more reasons than rainy days in Seattle why people in families get into the habit of hurting each other. I have grouped these reasons under four headings: cultural environment, individual temperament, mental disorders, and family legacies.

The cultural environment surrounding a family provides an uneven diet of support and distress. Leo and the other children of Roosevelt Towers woke up every day to a neighborhood filled with risk and ugliness as well as love and determination. Children and families in beautiful and affluent neighborhoods can get into trouble, too, because there are many family problems money alone can't solve and because of our culture's way of undermining loving and respectful relationships.

The second category of potential trouble is individual temperament. From birth we are active, calm, inquisitive, rambunctious, easy, or difficult. Mothers often know what a child's temperament will be like while the baby is still in the womb. Some children right from the start are mellow or anxious or easily frustrated as a part of who they are. This is nobody's fault, but it makes parenting a lot more complicated when a child's or a parent's temperament is difficult and especially when temperaments in a family tend to clash.

The third heading is mental disorders—depression or substance abuse, for example—which introduce a whole range of new problems. I recently met with a family where the older brother, because of his recent low energy and loss of interest in his close friends, was thought to be depressed. However, I could hardly complete the interview for the pell-mell activity of his three-year-old sister, who was into everything. Their mom said to me, "Oh, yes, she's been like that since she first starting kicking in the womb. There were many nights before and after she was born when I couldn't get any sleep until she fell asleep." This little girl may well be diagnosed with attention deficit disorder once she is in school. Untreated, disorders like these create situations that don't seem to respond to the usual solutions. For many of these conditions you will need specialized help.

The fourth heading is family legacies—our early childhood experiences that shape how we think and feel in family-like settings. If your parents routinely yelled at you, then their legacy to you is an urge to yell at your own children. If your parents were calm and loving all the time, then a calm and loving response to your own children will surface automatically. We learn how to parent from our parents for better and worse.

Throughout the book, the stories of three families, based on my many encounters with families in crisis, illustrate some of the ways that families get into trouble and how they can get out. These families include

- The McGraths, who struggled to end the resentment between them
- Margaret Hazen, whose efforts to be a good mother were hindered by a disorder she didn't know she had
- The Durrens, who show that even healthy families get into trouble sometimes

As you meet these families, notice how the parents contribute to the problems their children act out and how they learn to change and heal. Notice, too, how the children frequently offer helpful new perspectives on their family's distresses. If you try to see family conflicts through the eyes of your children, you will realize how parents repeatedly start fights without consciously meaning to do so.

Once, two middle-school-aged brothers were dragged to my office by their parents, who were worried by their boys' recent and persistent misbehavior. When I asked the parents to leave the room, the boys readily told me that their parents were talking about separating and they were scared and angry about it. Children often act out their objections when they feel their family is threatened. If, for example, parents suffer from alcoholism and refuse to recognize it, then they should expect an outcry from their children. No outcry at all would be more alarming—the children may be too frightened or too depressed to respond.

Many of the examples of family problems shared here are more severe than most of us will ever experience. Be thankful for that. But also learn from the starker examples so that the more subtle ones in your own family become easier to see. And keep in mind that these problems may be those of your neighbors or coworkers or the families of your children's friends. There is a world of hurt hiding behind designer doors and luxury cars as well as in workaday bungalows and shanties of poverty.

Your broken family will mend when you develop a plan and carry it out faithfully. But don't be fooled—you will have to work very hard to create a new atmosphere of happiness, love, and understanding in your family. This book will provide you with encouragement, inspiration, and direction to keep you on track.

A Note about How to Use This Book

This book is an introductory guide to solving difficult family problems. I wrote it for isolated, overwhelmed parents who need inspiration and ideas in order to organize a campaign for positive change in their families. If I can reach bewildered and frustrated parents with a message of hope and ideas that work, then parents with lesser distress will benefit, too. Real change in a family starts when one person (usually a parent) says, "Enough!" That's why Step 1 is about accepting responsibility. Step 2 helps you to identify the roots of your family's conflict and is a basic course in how families get into trouble. Step 3 is about getting ready for the campaign you choose to undertake by first putting your own life in order. Step 4 discusses basic good parenting strategies and ways to overhaul a chronically tense or hurtful family environment. Step 5 explores when and where to seek help. Step 6 presents basic information and encouragement to build your social support network, without which your family problems will become bigger and more difficult. Step 7 explores ways to find meaning and inspiration in the world immediately around you so you have the energy to create the changes you want. Step 8 provides more help with negotiating difficult relationships and ends with an inspirational story. In addition, the seven appendices provide information for further study and special help.

I recommend reading through the entire book and then going back and studying the parts where you recognize your family's situation. Not every strategy or solution will fit your particular situation. Look for answers to your questions, new ideas, and new sources of energy to tackle the trouble you face. Be gentle with yourself. Remember that nothing about good parenting is simple or easy. The book will help you find effective ways to gain cooperation from family members so you can heal old wounds and deal with the problems you've inherited from your family and community. My goal is to help you find real solutions to your problems, to nurture your confidence, and to encourage you to reach out to others who need help, too.

Families facing any of the more serious difficulties addressed in this book may not realize good help is available. They may need extended family, friends, teachers, pastors, or others to offer hope and show them change is possible. I hope that after you read this book and find the help you need, you will recommend it to another hurting family.

I realize that other cultures raise healthy children differently. I welcome input that helps translate essential truths about loving and respectful parenting into other cultural contexts. Contact me through my Web site at www.FamilyHealing.com.

A note of caution: As hard as I've worked to make family healing easier for you, doing the work in your own family will be up to you. You will need to translate other people's ideas and advice into strategies for your own family. Experiment with new ideas for as long as it takes to find the ones that really help your family. And if you need professional help, be sure you get it. This or any other book is no substitute for a careful evaluation of situations where the problems just won't go away. If you persevere through better and worse, then in time you, too, will celebrate the joy of a healthy family.

As a warmup, take the following quiz to find out how far you have already come on the road to healthy parenting.

After the questionnaire is a summary of the eight steps to family healing that are then developed in the eight parts that follow.

QUESTIONNAIRE

This questionnaire asks about some of your parental strengths and shortcomings. Answer honestly, then turn to appendix A and compare your answers to mine. Doing so will give you a better idea about how I approach these issues throughout the book.

1. I want to be a good parent.   Yes   No

2. I love my children no matter how badly they
    misbehave.   Yes   No

3. I feel out of control with my children too much
    of the time.   Yes   No

4. My parents gave me good models for how to be a
    good parent.   Yes   No

5. My ideas for dealing with trouble usually help
    make the situation better.   Yes   No

6. I can enjoy rebellious children.   Yes   No

7. I can be firm with my children when I need to be.   Yes   No

8. I can redirect my children from their misbehavior
    most of the time.   Yes   No

9. I can get my family to solve problems together.   Yes   No

10. My natural tendency is to give my child a second
    chance.   Yes   No

11. My children can make me laugh.   Yes   No

12. Sometimes I dread being with one or more of
    my children.   Yes   No

13. I have physically or mentally injured one of my
    children.   Yes   No

14. I can predict when trouble is likely to erupt in my family.   Yes   No

15. My partner and I work well together in raising our children.   Yes   No

16. There are alcoholics in my family.   Yes   No

17. Serious depression or anxiety problems run in my family.   Yes   No

18. I had some very rough times with my own parents.   Yes   No

19. Someone in my own family was sexually or physically abused.   Yes   No

20. I would seek professional help if I thought my family needed it.   Yes   No

21. My parents encourage my efforts to be a good parent.   Yes   No

22. I have a supportive extended family available to help me.   Yes   No

23. I have supportive friends who sometimes join in my family activities.   Yes   No

24. I have meaningful friends and activities of my own, separate from my family.   Yes   No

25. I belong to a community of people where I feel safe and accepted.   Yes   No

26. My family belongs to a community of faith or mutual support.   Yes   No

27. I notice beauty when I encounter it.   Yes   No

(continued on next page)

QUESTIONNAIRE *(continued)*

28. I find life miraculous at times.	Yes	No
29. I can raise healthy children.	Yes	No
30. I believe I am a good parent.	Yes	No

EIGHT STEPS TO ENDING FAMILY CONFLICT

Step 1—*Accept responsibility to lead your family's journey to health.*

Family healing starts when someone in the family sees the need for change and commits to finding and pursuing healthy solutions.

Step 2—*Identify the roots of your family's conflict.*

Healing requires that you identify the sources of your family's troubles.

Step 3—*Put your own life in order first.*

Find the courage to start fixing whatever is broken within yourself first, then you can effectively help your family.

Step 4—*Create the family culture you want.*

Old habits die hard. To end bad habits, families need compelling new ways to get along. Mutual respect, good humor, and generous listening must replace intimidation, humiliation, and getting even.

Step 5—*Ask for help.*

Raising children is no job for loners. The more severe the problems in your family, the more you will benefit from calling on others for help.

Step 6—*Find friends for yourself and your family.*
Involvement with other people who care about you and share your values reinforces your healing, strengthens your commitments to healthy family living, and enriches the experience of parenthood.

Step 7—*Pursue spiritual health.*
Create meaning and energy for your family's emotional and spiritual growth through celebrating together life's exquisite preciousness.

Step 8—*Refuse to give up.*
Rely on your own best judgment about what to try next, and seek help from others you trust. Find the love and stamina you need and you will bring happiness to your family.

STEP 1

ACCEPT RESPONSIBILITY TO LEAD YOUR FAMILY'S JOURNEY TO HEALTH

Family healing starts when someone in the family sees the need for change and commits to finding and pursuing healthy solutions.

WHERE DOES AN overwhelmed parent begin?

Mark avoided difficult conversations by disappearing into his basement workshop or staying away from home. His wife, Julie, had to cope with parents who still criticized every little mistake she made. Mark and Julie's young teenage daughter was spending time with friends her parents didn't trust. Their sixth-grade son spent his time glued to his video game, slaughtering anything that moved. These parents frequently felt powerless and frustrated and the children did their best to escape family tensions.

Taking responsibility for healing your family can feel lonely and bewildering. If you were an overwhelmed parent and I were your best friend, I would remind you that all parenting is difficult—there's nothing easy about it—and I would offer to comfort you with a hug. Then I'd take you to a really pleasant place and pamper you while you rested and regained your sense of humor. We would find a place for you to yell as loudly as you needed. (Yelling by yourself or with a friend can be very satisfying and perhaps make you too hoarse to yell at your family.) And I would listen—for as long as you needed me to listen—while you talked out your frustration and brainstormed ways to make the situation better.

Maybe you have a friend who could support you in ways like this. Or perhaps you know a doctor or priest or counselor or someone else you could ask for support. You might need to begin by making a telephone call or writing a letter. Someone will have to create a healing atmosphere at home. If not you, then who?

Chapter 1

GETTING STARTED

I know parents whose lives overwhelm them. One young father confided just one week after his first child was born that the very idea of dealing with family problems petrified him. A mother told me that every time her four children fought with each other, she felt desperate. Like all parents, they wanted their families to be healthy, but they were convinced they were helpless to bring about change. Be assured that stressed-out parents can find the vision and the energy they need to make the relationships in their families satisfying for everyone.

How Change Begins

Our families begin to heal the moment one of us decides to change. A young mother I knew was in the grocery store with her screaming four-year-old when she decided this time to pick up her furious son and walk out of the store. She noticed knowing smiles from other parents as she left. Her decision to create change rather than accept another tantrum was a radical departure from her customary helplessness. When we are determined to change, the usual ways we mistreat each other will no longer feel so acceptable or so inevitable.

Our own behavior leads the way to family change. For example, the next time our normal response would be to snap "Stop whining!" or "You stupid little jerk!" to stop a child's unwanted behavior, we can choose to say something respectful, positive, and encouraging instead.

- "Stop whining!" becomes "I know you want my attention. Wait one more minute. Then I will focus only on you."
- "You stupid little jerk!" can be rephrased "I am listening carefully now. Slow down and tell me again what you need."

Acting with reliable love and respect toward everyone within your troubled family gives you a sturdy foundation for change. If you consistently discipline yourself to say only encouraging and caring words to your children, they will usually reward you with cooperation. The few times they don't could be a test of their own independence or their responses to messages you don't realize you're expressing. Whatever they do, treat them lovingly, respect their integrity, and listen to them with your fullest attention. Figure out what they need and help them to find it.

It's Up to Us to Fix Our Own Unhappiness

The more childhood hurts we carry into adulthood, the more difficult it will be to be a good parent. Brian's father left when he was three years old and he had no helpful model for dealing with his defiant five-year-old. I observed another father slap his three-year-old son on the cheek when he misbehaved, and I wondered how this little boy will handle his children when he grows up. Our own early experiences with mistreatment are not our fault, but each of us is responsible now to figure out how to bring out the best of our parenting abilities in spite of less than ideal models.

Although others may have injured or humiliated us, each of us makes choices every day about how to handle these childhood experiences. By accepting responsibility, we shift the focus to making ourselves happy instead of feeling helpless and miserable.

Even though someone may provoke us, we choose how we respond. A colicky baby may make our frustration level rise, but she still needs calm and loving steadiness from us. So does our angry teenager or ten-year-old or our partner. We don't have to respond in anger or give up in exasperation. Instead, we can respond in a loving and respectful way.

Kenny McGrath slowly realized that he had to soften his own stubbornness and stop his excessive drinking or he would lose his second family. The learning process begins when we start to see our contributions to the tension in the family. We need to be gentle and forgiving with ourselves as we learn new ways to cope.

THE MCGRATH FAMILY'S STORY

Kenny McGrath was so shy and socially awkward that the first time Jeanne drove into his gas station, he couldn't say a word to her. She liked him immediately but, out of her own nervousness, didn't look at him when she paid for the gas. Kenny married someone else and had two children. His marriage fell apart eight years later because of his heavy drinking. Kenny and Jeanne met again by chance and started dating. When Jeanne got pregnant with Sarah, they chose to get married. Their son, Rusty, was born four years later. They struggled throughout their marriage over many issues, especially Kenny's excessive drinking and Jeanne's temper. Talking about feelings remained hard for them.

Two years ago Jeanne finally told Kenny to leave. Through two years of separation, Kenny stubbornly refused to stop drinking because, by his account, he resented being told what to do. Early in the separation Jeanne got involved with a teacher she'd known for years and had a baby boy she named Stevie. At that point Kenny realized that Jeanne would divorce him and he would lose Sarah and Rusty if he didn't accept responsibility for his drinking. Jeanne agreed to meet with him in family therapy in my office on his promise to remain sober.

Jeanne: Kenny, I still love you, but I can't have you drinking around the kids or me anymore.

Kenny: I'm not doing it anymore.

Jeanne: You've said that before, you know.

Kenny: This time I mean it. I'm tired of being alone.

Jeanne: I don't know if you're here because you really want to be a responsible father or if you're just lonely and looking for someone to share your bed.

Dr. Hall: Kenny, what took you so long to realize you had to stop drinking?

Kenny: I don't like people telling me what to do. If I want to drink after work, that's my business.

Dr. Hall: Why do you think you acted that way?

Kenny: Maybe I was too stubborn for my own good. It didn't seem to matter what I did, she'd be on me for something.

Dr. Hall: Sounds like she is your excuse for things not working out.

Kenny: I can't seem to help it. I'm trying to do better. I'm not drinking now.

SUGGESTIONS FOR CHANGE. Focus on how precious your family is. You'll find motivation and energy when you think about your love and hope for your children. If you don't connect with their preciousness right away, imagine yourself holding the infant you have always wanted. You are just as precious yourself, no matter what detours your life has taken.

Chapter 2

YOU ARE RESPONSIBLE (BUT NOT TO BLAME) FOR YOUR FAMILY'S SUFFERING

Autobiography in Five Short Chapters
Portia Nelson[2]

CHAPTER ONE
I walk down the street.
There is a deep hole in the sidewalk.
I fall in.
I am lost. . . . I am helpless.
It isn't my fault.
It takes forever to find a way out.

CHAPTER TWO
I walk down the same street.
There is a deep hole in the sidewalk.
I pretend I don't see it.
I fall in again.
I can't believe I am in this same place.
But, it isn't my fault.
It still takes a long time to get out.

CHAPTER THREE
I walk down the same street.
There is a deep hole in the sidewalk.
I *see* it there.
I still fall in . . . it's a habit . . . but,
   my eyes are open.
I know where I am.

.

It is *my* fault.
I get out immediately.

CHAPTER FOUR
I walk down the same street.
There is a deep hole in the sidewalk.
I walk around it.

CHAPTER FIVE
I walk down another street.

There is no easy route to healing. The essential step is to assume personal responsibility for your own shortcomings so you have a chance to fix them. As the poem above illustrates, after a while it becomes your fault when you fall into the hole in the sidewalk. Kenny stayed stuck in unhealthy patterns until he decided himself that he should stop drinking.

The challenge of good parenting is to find the good parent within you and to develop that good parent with love and patience. Try your best to discover ideas and attitudes that are helpful. With practice, you can put these new ideas to use.

Even if you have difficult children and intolerable circumstances to work with, as a parent you are in charge of your family's emotional health. If your family is hurting, you may have to try several avenues before you find the type of help you think you need.

Nancy and Mike hadn't expected to get pregnant and weren't sure they wanted to marry. They decided to stay together and have the baby, who was diagnosed at age two with cystic fibrosis, a life-shortening disease that clogs the lungs. Their baby was in and out of the hospital, medical bills piled up, and they found themselves fighting every night.

Their daughter's pediatrician sent them to a counseling agency. A counselor there suggested that they consider divorce. Neither felt right about that suggestion or about the counselor, so they talked with a priest Mike knew. This man didn't counsel couples, so he referred them to a psychologist in his congregation. She seemed friendly, listened, and appeared to grasp their wish to remain a family. Over several months she was able to help them stop blaming each other and showed them how to set ground rules for conversations about thorny topics. The stresses remained high, but Nancy and Mike began to share the burdens, which made their difficulties manageable. Because they kept looking until they found the help they needed, they deepened their friendship and brought comfort and satisfaction back into their relationship.

If you need help, you will have to ask for it. Since not all help will turn out to be what you need, you may have to ask again, as Mike and Nancy did. If you give up, your family's chances for recovery will plummet. Someone has to take the reins, and you are the best and maybe the only candidate.

If your baby suddenly choked, wouldn't you try to dislodge the plug? If your family keeps choking on the same problems, stand up and say, "Stop! There must be a better way."

Bring a new atmosphere to your family. From anywhere you can, gather the courage to say, "I will learn to be consistently loving and respectful and help my family to do the same."

How to Stop Making Excuses

If you find yourself making the following kinds of excuses for why you cannot make changes in your family, read the replies. They can help anytime you need a pep talk.

1. *Nobody will listen to me.* Maybe people have learned to ignore you. Aesop in the boy-crying-wolf fable reminds us to keep our demands honest. If you demand that people listen to you and you have nothing helpful to say, then they will tune you out. Do

others expect you to be critical, boring, or shaming? Do you waste their time with nagging or complaining? Or are you a good listener, truly working to understand what is said to you? And do you have substantially helpful things to say when your advice is sought?

2. *Why does it have to be me?* You have to lead the way because apparently nobody else will make the effort. Beginning a process of true change in your family may leave you feeling isolated, unappreciated, exhausted, and even excluded from the family at first. But you must realize that your road to healing will carry you through this stage.

3. *I don't know what to do.* You need new ideas. This book is a good place to start. You can also seek help from other books and the counsel of friends, mentors, other parents, extended family members, counselors, and religious leaders.

4. *I could never make it work.* This could be true, but to assume it is true before you even consider new ideas and new resources to strengthen your position is to give into old "ghosts" telling you old fibs. Don't quit before you even start.

5. *I am not strong enough to solve such huge problems.* This, too, may be true for now. But remember that military recruits are not expected to be battle-ready on arrival at boot camp. Training, conditioning, and discipline all help ready us for strenuous tasks we would not otherwise be able to accomplish. Build your strength and confidence by looking for new ways to approach your problems. Discuss your ideas with others who can teach and encourage you. Keep an open mind about what you can accomplish. If you need a coach, enlist a friend, employ a counselor, or form an alliance where you and someone else agree to listen to each other.

6. *Nobody cares anyway.* If *you* care, then the statement is false. The journey may well be lonely for a time, but if you are determined to see change, change will follow. Don't give up.

7. *I can't stand to confront these problems.* If this is true, then you will not be able to create healing for your family. If you genuinely cannot tolerate facing your family's problems, if you are afraid of them, then you will need to rely on someone else. However, no matter how bad your problems are, this statement is probably false. Instead, you may be worried that you will feel horrible as you deal with these issues. Go back to excuse numbers 3, 4, and 5 and look into ways you can grow into someone who brings healing to your family.

Any Place You Choose to Start Can Work

The Serenity Prayer of Alcoholics Anonymous (AA), adapted from the original by Reinhold Neibuhr, offers clear direction to help us conquer our problems and find inner peace.

> God, grant me the Serenity to accept the things
> I cannot change,
> Courage to change the things I can,
> and the Wisdom to know the difference.

You can raise a healthy family! Admit that it will be hard and have the courage to face your family situation. Don't give in to old ideas about being helpless or worthless.

Say the following statement out loud:

I will do my best to take charge of my own and my family's emotional recovery.

Acquiring new skills and strategies to help your family get along will provide the antidote you need for the inevitable setbacks you will encounter along the way. You are the expert on your own family. One good idea can be enough to make a fresh start.

I once counseled a painfully shy single mother who was desperate to help her painfully shy first-grade daughter make a new friend. She chose to attend parent-teacher meetings in hopes of meeting a new friend for herself and her daughter. This may seem like a tiny step, but it was a beginning. When your intent is truly to make a situation better, you will nourish your family's soul and provide new hope for all of you, even if a particular attempt doesn't work out right away.

Initiating Change Is Often Lonely

As a rule, families don't like to change. Anyone trying to make changes will stir up trouble. For this reason, unhealthy families get stuck in unchanging roles. A healthy family, however, will be proud of each member's growing abilities and independence and accept the changes this growth usually brings. For example, Bobby was a handsome, but sometimes depressed, young teenager who shocked his religiously conservative parents when he told them he wanted to become a fashion model. Fortunately, their love outshone their misgivings and, after they were satisfied that the modeling agency was legitimate, they supported his tryouts.

Families stuck in cycles of conflict can find it very hard to change because old ways have become habits and unpleasant scenes are replayed over and over. Two-year-old Betsy felt displaced by her newborn brother, so she sought attention by pinching the baby and crying loudly about any minor injury. When her mother became pregnant again two years later, Betsy's aggressiveness got worse and so did her mother's frustration and helplessness. As Betsy felt more overtaken by jealousy, she would torment her little brother and had to be kept away from the new baby. When her father threatened to leave because of the tension at home, Betsy's fears grew stronger and her misbehavior grew worse. Breaking a cycle of tension like this will take determined effort.

Families often become tied up in an emotional knot of anger and hurt feelings that no one seems able to untangle. Here's where somebody's vision and courage are needed to create space for change. In as caring a way as you can, challenge the hurtful old patterns and replace them with loving and respectful new ones. Set an example of the behavior you want your family to copy. When those who don't want to change resist, humor them respectfully, continue to invite them to change, and don't quit trying.

One Committed Person Can Create Family Change

The more serious the problems, the more deeply committed and persistent a change-seeking parent must be—single-minded, steel-willed, even fanatic. One person who believes strongly enough in the possibility of healing will in time convert the skeptics and expose those unwilling to change.

Jeanne McGrath took four years to accumulate the strength to tell Kenny to leave. Her mother could not give Jeanne and the three children a home and neither could Jeanne's friends. The added expense of setting up a second household was beyond their means, so Jeanne went to work as a part-time receptionist. To his credit, Kenny continued to maintain a steady income despite his heavy after-hours drinking.

Jeanne: When I first told Kenny he had to leave if he didn't stop drinking, he sobered up for a while. He was furious with me, though, and it wasn't too long before he went back to drinking, almost like he needed to prove he could do whatever he wanted.

Kenny was drinking so heavily then that despite feeling guilty about letting his children down, he wasn't able to stop himself.

Sarah finally got her daddy's attention. While trying to make cook-ies with Kenny's help, she tipped over a flour tin. He yelled at her to be more careful. She snapped back, "You're just a dumb daddy!"

According to Kenny, that comment was a turning point. "What she said was true," he told me. It took a while, but the night the truth sank in Kenny went to his first AA meeting in years.

SUGGESTIONS FOR CHANGE. As an experiment, stop taking part in any family squabbles for a day (or an hour, if a day seems too long for you). Instead, stay calm, keep your sense of humor, and do something distracting like singing or smiling or talking about the weather or your grandmother or the cat. A joke can sometimes ease the stress:

Knock, knock.
Who's there?
Orange.
Orange who?
Orange you glad we're not yelling anymore?

During the calm, do some research about how to prolong the peace and shorten the family wars. Read this book and others from the suggested reading list in appendix D. Ask a friend or your doctor for input. Promise yourself you won't take part in family arguments. Tell someone you trust that you are ending your part in fueling these recurrent battles of will. If it makes sense to do so, enlist his or her help.

Believe in Yourself

Jeanne felt stuck for years because she had very young children, poor support from her own family, and limited money. She eventually realized that what she lacked was not support or money but courage and a plan. Believing we can make a difference can create the incentives and energy that make change possible.

Looking at problems in new ways can generate new ideas to solve them. Imagine new strategies and find the courage to test them.

After their separation, Kenny and Jeanne both feared more failure. In my office they struggled to reconnect with each other.

Jeanne: You scare all of us when you drink. I can't trust you.

Kenny: I told you I'm sorry. I'm sober now. What more do you want?

Jeanne: The kids are having a hard time without you. But I still worry about them when they're with you.

Kenny: (his irritation showing) Look, I know I'm not perfect. All I know is, I love you, I love my kids, and I think we ought to be together. You have to trust me.

Jeanne: I'm trying.

Their progress was painfully slow, but Jeanne and Kenny did manage to rekindle the love that brought them together and began again to build the trust they needed to reunite their family.

For all of you struggling to break out of painful old patterns, I have added a sixth chapter to the poem at the beginning of this chapter:

CHAPTER SIX

The new street is unfamiliar.

I still feel lost . . . and afraid.

There is a deep hole in the sidewalk.

This time I fill it and sign it "Freedom!"

Now when I pass by,

I watch others celebrate my victory and their own.

STEP 2

IDENTIFY THE ROOTS OF
YOUR FAMILY'S CONFLICT

Healing requires that you identify the

sources of your family's troubles.

FAMILY PROBLEMS THAT don't get better have roots hidden in family history or someone's genes or both. Finding where trouble starts helps you figure out what to do.

Early in my hospital training I met a world-weary grandmother with a lifelong history of depression who asked to be hospitalized to prevent another suicide attempt. She recalled feeling the same way a generation ago, when her daughter was the age of her granddaughter now. In a group meeting, the doctor asked if anything had happened to *her* at that age, and she suddenly started to sob. When she could speak again, she told the group that her stepfather had molested her at that same age. She had not remembered it until the question was asked. For the next several days she cried and raged. Then she left the hospital with a joy and peace she'd not known since age four.

Before the next argument or shouting match in your family, write down your answers to these questions:

- What are the conflicts in my family that keep coming back?
- Where does each conflict come from?
- Who starts each conflict and who keeps it going?
- Does someone's mood, behavior, or temperament add to the difficulties?

Questions that go to the roots of a conflict open new doors and highlight possible solutions. The next four chapters will guide you in creating good questions and searching for answers.

Chapter 3

CURRENT CULTURE
AND INDIVIDUAL TEMPERAMENT

Family troubles come from four principal sources, like major roots of a tree: (1) current culture (the world around us), (2) individual temperament (our personalities), (3) mental disorders (physical conditions), and (4) family legacies, or "ghosts" (events from our past that still haunt us). This chapter will cover the first two, which are sources of trouble for every family, no matter how healthy.

Current Culture and the Society We Live In

Stresses in our day-to-day lives provide plenty of sparks to ignite conflict. Family trouble can develop from any stressful situation. The best of parents will lose control sometimes—to a squalling baby, a cranky child, or a sullen teenager. What we may have difficulty recognizing are the ways the culture around us can make the situation worse.

Stephen Glenn and Jane Nelsen point out that the economic boom in America since World War II, including the ever-rising influence of television, has seriously compromised the opportunities for our children to learn traditional values, such as respect for elders, cooperation, hard work, persistence, and mutual support.[3] Family networks have steadily eroded as both parents have been forced to work, divorce has left more single parents trying to cope alone, and television and video games have preempted family and friendship time with a mind-numbing diet of sexual stimulation, violent responses to conflict, and combative heroes. The result is children filled with feelings and ideas about life and themselves based on fantasy and advertising rather than on their own family's values and traditions.

John Nichols and Robert McChesney point out how corporate mergers in the late 1990s have delivered the control of America's mainstream media into the boardrooms of nine multinational corporations, accelerating a trend toward increased commercialization of the media at the expense of public conversations on important issues and public policy. They note a study that shows how media influences our children: presented with otherwise identical shoes labeled "Nike" or "Kmart," eight-year-olds liked them both, whereas twelve-year-olds scoffed at the Kmart logo.[4] A constant television, radio, newspaper, and billboard message to buy can create enormous pressures on parents.

Dr. Mary Pipher believes American culture is "at war with families" in the United States today. The media, especially television, are educating our children to be consumers and exposing them to adult fare without our permission. The news media highlight violence and sex to get our attention so advertisers can tell us what to buy. One consequence of this "cultural war" is the dissolution of our sense of community. Some of us feel we can't even be friendly with children we don't know because to be a stranger who smiles or plays with children might lead to a misunderstanding. Such need for caution diminishes the mutual support we can offer each other and isn't healthy for our children or us.[5]

One area of mental and emotional disability that may receive substantial contributions from current culture is eating disorders. The anorectic supermodel "Twiggy" made a huge international splash in the late 1960s, and many warnings were issued to girls who strove to emulate her gaunt appearance. Similarly, the "waif" look of the 1990s, epitomized by ultraslender model Kate Moss, sparked new controversy about girls' and women's body images. In a 1998 survey of body measurements of 500 professional agency models, Professor Patricia Owen of St. Mary's University in San Antonio, Texas, found that over three-quarters of these models were medically underweight and nearly one quarter of them were at least 15 percent below normal body weight (a criterion along with self-starvation, for a diagnosis of anorexia nervosa).[6] These are the women hired to model clothes and sell products on television.

If we as parents fail to provide the love and direction our children need to evaluate cultural risks, then they become vulnerable to the amoral lure of self-indulgence and quick fixes, peer substitutes for family, and apathy. We need to give our children a major infusion of our love every day and model our values for them consistently.

One way to sharpen our awareness of our children's exposure to our culture is to ask questions like these:

- Whose values are our children demonstrating in their current behavior?
- Who is guiding and stimulating their growing minds?
- What do they do for entertainment besides watch television and play video games?
- Where are places children can gather for group games and conversation?
- Who is providing the resources they need for creative play and projects?

SUGGESTIONS FOR CHANGE. Have a family discussion about culture, society, and values and how they impact each of you in the family. Talk about expectations you and your children have now and for the future. Talk about what makes each person genuinely happy. Discuss family finances, jobs, school, and time together. Talk about neighbors and friends, what's popular and what's not. Talk about interesting news reports. If you have trouble getting started, try asking what impact television, friends, or video games have on what each child chooses to wear, who they want to be like, and what they want to buy.

Practice listening. Elicit opinions, information, and new ideas. Discourage arguments by setting ground rules.

Temperament

Our personalities (for example, bold or timid, moody or mellow) affect the way we each experience the world. We are individuals with a wide range of abilities to feel pain, joy, fear, empathy, and excitement. Children, even twins, are born different. Children with temperaments that clash with those of their family or who are difficult to soothe create tensions for the whole family that can make effective parenting seem impossible. Temperamental parents make their own lives more difficult when they do not learn to moderate their reactions. To parent well, we must orchestrate a harmonious blend of the individual temperaments in our family.

Research tells us that about one-third of our children are more difficult to parent because of irritability, moodiness, distractibility, high energy, curiosity, fearfulness, shyness, and other traits. Healthy parenting will help these more vulnerable children learn to cope with these traits. The extra effort and attention difficult children require, however, can overwhelm a family. Divorce and remarriage add additional stresses that tend to bring out these underlying difficulties.

I met Renee and Shawn soon after their youngest daughter entered school. Renee resumed her nursing career and Shawn shifted his work schedule to be home after school. They were frustrated with six-year-old Colleen, who insisted on coming into their bed at night. Their efforts to return her to her own bed were met with tears and tantrums.

GROUND RULES FOR
A FAMILY DISCUSSION

Gather at the best time for everyone to get together (this may take some negotiating) and sit so everyone can see everyone else—often a circle is best. The person who asked for the discussion then opens the conversation by summarizing what the discussion will be about and setting the limit on how long each person will speak. Once everyone agrees what the discussion is about, begin sharing ideas and opinions.

One person speaks at a time. Everyone else listens. (If you like, use the Native American tradition of passing a "talking stick" around. The one with the stick has everyone else's attention until he or she passes the stick to someone else, who is then the only one to talk, until everyone has a turn.)

Each person speaks only for herself or himself.

Everyone abides by the time limits set for each speaker and for the entire discussion.

No one makes personal attacks or uses violence.

All family members respect the rights of others to their own opinions. If discussions break down into arguments, take a time-out. Ask those who are arguing to write down their ideas for a later gathering.

This assignment is designed to help them break the habit of attacking each other. If anyone is unhappy with the way a discussion is led, that person can call another meeting later and lead that discussion.

We reviewed the problem from Colleen's perspective and reasoned that this was Colleen's way to make sure she wasn't losing her parents' love. Three months of patient, reassuring parenting didn't make Colleen an easy child, but it did reduce her tantrums and kept her sleeping in her own bed.

Mismatched temperaments between parents and children are a big risk in adoptive families as well as biological families. A gregarious and aging professional couple had a first baby who turned out to be exceptionally shy and sensitive. She startled easily and cried nearly every time her parents took her into public places. When I met them, the parents were frustrated and restless because of the limitations their daughter had imposed on their social lives. My contribution was to reassure them that their baby's fussiness was not their fault and to help them accept the inevitable loss of freedom a child imposes on new parents.

Inborn Temperament

Each of us at conception is dealt an assortment of biological attributes that affect who we become. Gender, race, intelligence, agility, and mood all have roots in the genes we get from our biological parents. Whether these traits blend into a functional personality depends on how we are nurtured through early and middle childhood.

Some children create instant anxiety in adults by their rambunctious disregard for danger. They climb anything, dart everywhere, and scare anyone who's watching. Others are as mellow as sunning house cats. Both kinds "teach" adults around them how to behave—always on edge or calm and at ease. Once you learn to spot it, there's humor in seeing how readily children trigger the responses of unsuspecting adults. It reminds me of the bumper sticker that warns, "Insanity is inherited. You get it from your children."

An early "failure" in my practice was a young family who brought me their incorrigibly defiant and aggressive four-year-old. The child seemed healthy to me, albeit very active and headstrong, so I reassured the parents they were doing a good job and simply needed to persevere in loving her and setting stable limits. They cancelled the follow-up appointment and I didn't hear back from them. Two years later I had some free time and called the family to find out what I did to scare them away. The mother told me our session had changed everything. They started to see their daughter as a remarkable child instead of a troubled one, and she was now flourishing.

Maintain a No-Fault Perspective on Your Family's Problems

A child who *never* gets along doesn't know how. Children whose social styles clash with those around them need to learn new social skills. Parents of a difficult child may well need to learn special parenting skills.

Alex was in the fifth grade when his principal suspended him for hitting a classmate. At home, his older brother routinely told him to "get lost." When asked if he had any close friends, Alex said no. He said that other kids didn't want to play with him. Alex's mother said Alex was always more difficult to get along with than anyone else in the family. He routinely complained about other people mistreating him but wouldn't admit when he started trouble. Other children found him hard to play with because he bent the rules to make sure he won. When other children came to his house, he'd yell at them when they didn't follow his frequently changing rules. After one or two visits most of his peers refused to play with him anymore. At school they started making fun of him ("Alex is a spoilsport!" and "Who'd want to play with him?") and excluded him from their group games.

Alex's complaining and ready temper made him an easy target for teasing. Children like Alex often don't know how to get along with their peers. They lack empathy. Other children don't like to play with them because it's no fun being with someone who makes you feel bad. Children like Alex need to learn to see themselves as others see them. They need to learn social skills that help them negotiate what to play and how to play cooperatively with other children.[7]

SUGGESTIONS FOR CHANGE. Imagine what the world looks like through the eyes of your most difficult child. How does he or she experience the conflicts in your family? Pay special attention to how you think this child sees you. If you're not sure, and even if you think you are sure, ask your child directly. Then tailor your nurturing and discipline to the ways this child sees and reacts.

Carrie was a wonderful eight-year-old who loved school and sulked at home. Her mother tried to cheer her up. When that didn't work, she said some unkind words, which Carrie answered with tears and more sulking. Soon her mother brought her to me.

Carrie's twelve-year-old sister was a gifted child who clearly overshadowed Carrie at home. Carrie had come to believe her parents didn't love her as much as they loved her sister and so she sulked. When her mother tried to cheer her up, Carrie felt her mother was only pretending to like her. And when her mother got angry with her, Carrie knew for sure her mother liked her sister more.

When she understood what caused Carrie's sulking, her mother then knew she had to help Carrie see herself as special just for being Carrie, not in comparison to anyone else. "I can see how you would think that Daddy and I love your sister best," she said. "We're very proud of her. But we're very proud of you, too. We love you. You are the only one in the world who can bring us Carrie joy because you're the only Carrie in the world."

Respect each child's point of view as you show him or her better ways to get along. Loving and respectful parenting helps children to cope with the traits they were born with.

How to Distinguish Inborn from
Acquired Personality Traits

The longer and more consistently a child has behaved with certain tendencies, the more likely these tendencies are inborn, especially if the child's problems are distinctly different from those of other children in the same family. I commonly hear stories about an aunt or uncle or grandparent who was very much like the child whose current behavior is cause for concern. What wisdom or warning can you glean from relatives about what to anticipate as your child grows up?

Watch for the child's responses to different situations. Can the child get along well under some conditions and seem an outcast in others? What determines the difference? At his or her best, how well can the child do? Tasks that a child never masters are probably beyond reach for now. Help the child to make choices that promise success.

Laurie sometimes got so wrapped up in her fantasy play in kindergarten that she would walk right through the play of other children. Early in the school year, the other children teased her and sometimes hit her. Her teacher helped her to be more aware of her surroundings and helped her classmates to alert her before she wrecked their play.

If the teacher's assumption had been that Laurie was clumsy or intentionally disruptive, then Laurie's inattention likely would have been greeted with anger and insults by the other children and punishments from her teacher. Reactions such as these could make Laurie's behavior worse—for example, she might start ruining other children's games on purpose.

The fact that a child is disruptive or argumentative does not mean the child chooses to be that way. As often as not, the child simply doesn't know how to behave more cooperatively. Therein lies the opportunity for learning new skills that can get better results.

Chapter 4

MENTAL DISORDERS

Biologically based mental disorders, the third major root of persistent family conflict, play a big role in the pain of many families. If you are reading this book because problems in your family just don't seem to get better, then an understanding of biological disorders of the brain may prove crucial to figuring out what's wrong and finding the help you need. Accurate identification of these sometimes subtle but always disruptive problems can open up doors to effective new help you won't find any other way. At least consider the idea that a family member could be suffering with a mental disorder.

Diagnosing someone with a mental disorder is the job of a trained professional, such as your family doctor, a psychiatrist, or a psychologist. Noticing the signs of a possible mental disorder and seeking help are up to you.

Whenever a person's competence or good humor seems to be missing for long periods of time, a mental disorder may be present. If this has been a lifelong problem, it may seem normal, when in fact it is a sign of a treatable disorder. Members of a family who continually display irritable, angry, sullen, impulsive, or repetitive behavior may be depressed, anxious, addicted, or in some other way afflicted with a disorder that keeps them from consistently returning the love and respect they receive.

Too often people suffer for years before seeking help or the help they do receive is not appropriate for them. Once they arrive in my office, I am usually able to help them feel much better in a relatively short period of time. Every month or two I evaluate another survivor of long-term psychotherapy for depression who gets better for the first time in years within weeks of starting to take an appropriate medication. This is not to detract from the benefit of talking out your problems. That can be essential, but it may not be sufficient if the bio-logically based depression or anxiety is severe.

Mental disorders refer to brain-based problems with how we function and how we feel. Symptoms of mental disorders signifi-cantly disrupt our lives. For example, a child refuses to go to school because his anxiety is so high when he leaves home that he cannot pay attention to his teacher or friends. A parent has to sneak a drink in the morning to quell his anxieties about leaving for work. These problems might run in the family for many generations or show up out of the blue.

Typically, mental disorders cause behavior that comes between people, damages self-esteem, and disrupts a person's ability to cope with life's problems. Mental disorders keep a person from perform-ing at his or her usual level of competence. A small group of mental disorders cause people to lose their connection with reality. More common examples of disabilities are clinical depression, panic anxi-ety, and substance abuse.

A major study of mental disorders in the United States in 1992 found that 48 percent of the randomly sampled population ages fif-teen to fifty-four reported symptoms that met the diagnostic criteria for at least one mental disorder during their lifetime.[8] Depression, substance abuse, and anxiety made up about 60 percent of the total. The National Institute on Alcohol Abuse and Alcoholism estimated that in 1992 alone, 5½ million Americans met the diagnostic criteria for alcohol abuse or alcohol dependence.[9] That means their alcohol use caused significant health, family, or work-related problems. (See appendix B for detailed information.)

The impact of severe depression, alcoholism, or anxiety on a family can be enormous. Earlier we met Kenny McGrath, whose alcoholic behavior ruined one marriage and nearly ruined another. Someone in your own family or a neighbor probably struggles with a mental disorder. An active mental disorder affects someone in virtually every three-generation family.

The whole idea of a mental disorder is very scary for many people. It is also very real for those who suffer a mental disorder and for their families. So please don't run away from it too quickly. Like diabetes or heart disease or cancer, mental disorders have a wide range of severity that goes from easily managed to life threatening.

Rather than ignoring symptoms or hoping they'll go away on their own, you will always do better facing a mental disorder directly, naming it accurately, and then deciding if and how you want to deal with it.

SUGGESTIONS FOR CHANGE. Look through the descriptions for common major mental disorders in appendix B to see if anyone in your immediate or extended family seems to fit the symptom picture of any of the disorders listed.[10] To qualify as a problem, a symptom has to be severe enough to significantly impair the person's ability to function competently and consistently at his or her appropriate developmental level.

If you find significant symptoms in members of your family, an early psychiatric evaluation could save your family oceans of ongoing frustration. See appendices C and F for further help.

MARGARET HAZEN'S STORY

Margaret Hazen's energy was infectious and I was quickly drawn into her story. She described herself as a "frazzled has-been track star" who was divorced with three children. The illness that had ended her athletic career had careened out of control again.

Margaret: Dr. Hall, you wouldn't believe what a mess I've made of my life. I should be a Nike executive or something. But look at me. I can't even get my kids off to school in the morning, much less run a company.

Approaching thirty, she seemed more like a teenager—nervous and giddy with hair mussed and clothes mismatched. A year ago she went back to work after her now ex-husband had been sent to jail on drug charges. Her baby, Lottie, was a poor sleeper and had been difficult to soothe for most of her first year. Jonathan had just turned eleven. He slept on the sofa of the family's one-bedroom apartment. Many nights he still wet himself. Fifteen-year-old Joey was often rude to his mother.

Margaret: You can't believe how hard it's been since the divorce. The kids refuse to do anything I say. They blame me for their daddy going away. The older ones call me the same names they heard their daddy say. The littlest things explode into tantrums. Joey's watching television and Jonathan or Lottie wants to watch, too, but they can't sit still and Joey gets mad because he wants to watch his show, so he hits them and they come crying to me. Then Joey yells at them to "shut up, you little crybabies." I cry myself to sleep at night after Lottie falls asleep in my bed.

Dr. Hall: *(interrupting)* Margaret, tell me how you hope I
              can help you.

Margaret: I want to get my life in order. I'm frazzled all
             the time. I need to slow down. I need to plan
             things out. I can't even go to the grocery store
             and come back with what I went for. It's like
             God threw me into a dryer and I'm just tumbling
             all the time.

Through the tumble of her words I began to recognize the
speedy, nonstop speech pattern of a bipolar mood swing disorder (also called a manic-depressive mood swing disorder—
more information can be found in appendix B).

After a careful evaluation that included questions about her
symptoms, medical and mental health history, and family history, I recommended that she take medicine for her mood
swings, gave her a prescription for a mood-stabilizing medication, and set a return appointment. She came back after two
weeks on the medicine. "I can't believe I feel so much better,"
she said. Over the following weeks she found a toddlers group
through her local community center and started to make
supportive new friends.

Medicines sometimes provide a magic lift out of the mire of mental disability. When they work, they make it much easier for us to
address our other problems and think through possible solutions.

Like a major long-term medical disorder or developmental disability, a chronic mental disorder for one member of a family will
cause high levels of stress for the whole family. This is obvious during
the acute phases of an illness. Less obvious but even more stressful
may be the long-term emotional wear and tear.

A Special Plea to Seek Treatment
for Depression

Depression is more common than heart disease, causes potentially severe disability, and can be lethal. Yet depression is a very treatable disorder. Psychiatry and psychology together have achieved a nearly 90 percent remission rate for those who pursue a full range of treatment options.

SYMPTOMS OF CLINICAL DEPRESSION

Clinical depression is a medical illness that causes physical problems with sleep, appetite, energy, thinking, motivation, and mood. You may well suffer from depression if you experience most of the following symptoms for more than a week or if you experience them frequently for several months:

- Trouble sleeping or sleeping too much
- Poor appetite or eating too much
- Low energy during the day
- Poor concentration
- Low motivation
- More irritability than usual
- Loss of enjoyment of activities you ordinarily enjoy
- Lowered sexual energy and interest
- Hopelessness
- Persistent thoughts of dying or killing yourself

In the United States, one in three to four women and one in eight to ten men will experience this level of clinical depression at least once in their lifetime.[11] Please see your physician if there is any possibility you might be depressed.

SUGGESTIONS FOR CHANGE. Follow the three suggestions below for two months and your mild to moderate depression should ease or disappear:

- *Daily aerobic exercise* that elevates your heart rate for twenty to thirty minutes — brisk walking, for example — can bring impressive recovery over several months for many forms of anxiety, mild to moderate depression, and many mild to moderate medical ailments. Work your way up from shorter workouts to longer ones as you get in better shape.

- Engage in *regular activities that leave you feeling better* about yourself, and eliminate activities that leave you feeling worse about yourself. For example, find a few minutes to work at a hobby you enjoy or play music that makes you feel good as you go about your tasks. Stay away from coworkers who are overly critical and turn off the evening news if it bothers you.

- *Supportive self-talk* is clearly helpful. One popular form of therapy, called "cognitive behavioral therapy," teaches ways to think in a more positive manner and thereby improve your mood. For example, instead of "I can't do it," say to yourself, "I know this will be hard, but I can take my time and do a little bit each day." If you hear yourself say, "I'm a total failure," tell yourself, "That's not true. Some of my plans have not worked out, but when I do my best and ask for help, I can succeed well enough." (See appendix D for suggested books on cognitive behavioral therapy.)

If regular use of these three strategies does not eliminate your depression, then your depression is probably too severe for these strategies alone. See your doctor. Medication may be your best next experiment.

Chapter 5

EMOTIONAL LEGACIES, OR "GHOSTS"

The fourth root of family conflict is the legacies we as parents carry, especially from early childhood.

A legacy is something handed down from one generation to the next. A keepsake and an inheritance are both legacies. When it comes to parenting skills, the legacies we are most concerned about are the feelings every one of us carries from earliest childhood. Our experiences with our own parents define for us what being a family feels like. When it's our turn to parent, these memories affect how we raise our children, often the same way our parents raised us. In this way, family traditions of love and comfort or shame and anger are reproduced for another generation. Since this process works largely without our realizing it, these legacies can be hard to change.

This notion of emotional legacies is the single most important idea new parents must master if they want to be truly in charge of the atmosphere in their own family. Painful legacies can be the hidden reasons parents are having so much trouble now. These troubling legacies from childhood, which I refer to as "ghosts," take away from the love and trust we have with our children.

The lesson here is a hard one: if we fail to remember and outgrow our own painful experiences from childhood, we set in motion a powerful and usually unconscious process that will recreate similar pain for our children.[12]

SUGGESTIONS FOR CHANGE. Write down your responses to the following questions so you can compare your answers today to your answers a month, six months, and a year from now.

- How often do I lose my temper with members of my family?
- How often do I say positive, supportive, and encouraging words to my children, as opposed to negative, critical, or shaming words?
- How often do I model the behavior I want from my children?
- Is the behavior I don't like in my children like that of anyone close to them or close to me recently or in the past?

Keep a daily diary of your feelings and reactions. Look closely for patterns in your responses and others' reactions. Within a week (or maybe a day) you should be able to see patterns in situations that arise repeatedly.

Pay special attention to the patterns that are working well. These are your patterns for success. Then focus on the patterns that are not working well. Choose a pattern that doesn't get the results you hope for, change your part in the sequence, and watch how others' reactions change. Monitor what happens. Keep improving your own actions until those around you start to follow suit or begin to complain that you have changed!

Parents' Legacies

Many experiences, especially early ones—the sudden loss of a loved one, a parent with mental illness, a life-threatening illness, divorce, persistent family patterns of interpersonal hostility, and other traumas—

can leave lasting scars. Perhaps your parents were overwhelmed by similar events so they were not able to provide all the love and attention you required.

If that was the case, you may need instruction in effective parenting. Because parenting requires a wide range of skills, what we don't learn from our parents and parental figures as we grow up, we need to learn elsewhere. Every new situation requires a new effort to figure it out. Uncertainty about what to do uses up our energy. Nowadays, helpful parenting classes teach many of these skills to parents who didn't learn them from their own parents.

Understanding Emotional Ghosts

Emotional ghosts create havoc in families. Learning to recognize them and then eliminate them plays a major part in healing family problems. The term "ghosts" refers to those unresolved legacies or emotional crises from early childhood that continue to disrupt our lives long after we have grown up. In effect, these upsetting experiences haunt us. That's why I use the term "ghosts."

"You are just like my mother!"

"Oh, you look just like your father!"

Sound familiar?

Our brains are hard-wired to compare events, especially ones that generate fear. From the beginning, human survival depended on our ability to learn from the dangers we survived and to apply that knowledge to new perils. Unfortunately, what is necessary for survival of life-threatening emergencies does not always foster the love and respect necessary for healthy families.

Unhealed Early Hurts Can Leave Emotional Scars

The greatest threats to our grown-up emotional integrity come during our earliest childhood years. Children rely on early experiences of love and safety to learn how to love, trust, and feel secure as adults. But many children do not experience reliable love and safety. The result is often an adult unable to trust intimate relationships or one who develops self-destructive habits as a way to cope. Verbal abuse can undermine a growing child's self-esteem. Any of these threats will affect the rest of a child's life, complicating every future stressful event.

Understanding this relationship helps us recover from the effects of childhood events. It's important to identify these outdated feelings, beliefs, and flashbacks, which interrupt our lives until we learn not to let them panic us. Once we recognize the patterns, we can face our ghosts directly.

Ghosts can be created in surprising ways. As a young teenager, I was riding in our family car with my newly licensed sister at the wheel when a huge double-trailer truck loaded with lumber loomed behind us, traveling at well over 70 miles an hour. (I was watching the speedometer from the back seat.) A movie flashed in my mind of the truck smashing into us, our car somersaulting down the freeway with lumber crashing through the car windows, and the car exploding in a ball of flames that killed us all. In fact, the trucker pulled safely past us and cruised out of sight. To this day, over forty years later, I must still remind myself to relax when I see a large lumber truck on the freeway. That truck created a ghost for me—a terrifying glimpse of death.

Any circumstance that makes a child feel helpless in the face of fear, humiliation, or abandonment can potentially create a ghost. Events as seemingly innocuous as changing schools repeatedly can create ghosts for a child who has difficulty integrating into new social settings. A man who as a child was bullied on the way to school may deep down still fear attack when he walks to work.

Ghosts usually operate behind the scenes of our daily lives, recreating feelings from our early lives that clash with the lives we are living today. Ghosts encourage us to act out old scripts, to say things that are at odds with our own best judgment. The more traumatic the experiences behind a ghost memory, the more likely the ghost will create ongoing conflicts in our lives. For example, a child who spent her elementary school years in a small school with the same teacher repeatedly shaming her in front of the class whenever she made a mistake will likely grow up to be highly anxious in any meeting where she might be humiliated.

Ghosts can also deceive us about how family members should treat each other, and they can set up expectations that being a family means someone has to misbehave in a certain way. In other words, someone who grew up experiencing a particular misbehavior—heavy drinking or angry outbursts, for example—can fall into similar patterns around their own children or choose a partner who does.

Jeanne and Kenny McGrath both had fathers who were alcoholics. Jeanne married Kenny despite knowing he drank too much, as her father had, and Kenny kept on drinking despite the problems his father's alcoholism had caused. Heavy drinking in a family was something they were used to. Their children also became victims of the family legacy of alcoholic behavior.

Chapter 6

How to Recognize Your Ghosts

Once you know what to look for, it's not difficult to tell when ghosts are affecting your behavior. Pay attention to your very first thoughts and feelings in any situation. They are often so automatic and so fleeting you don't even realize you have them. Listen for command words like "should," "never," "always," and "have to" in the phrases you say to yourself. These are clues that ghosts are at work. Pay attention if you feel trapped, intimidated, self-righteous, worthless, mistrustful, hopeless, humiliated, victimized, or overwhelmed. These are common ghost feelings. Terror and rage often leave us speechless, which may be why these particular feelings almost always generate ghost memories, often experienced as intensely painful emotions that well up for no apparent reason and with no words to describe them.

A capable young man was offered a promising job he had looked for months to find, but he turned it down because he couldn't find an affordable place to live that allowed him to commute by bicycle or bus. When this man was a small child, his father took him driving at high speeds that ended on three different occasions in accidents, one of which landed him in the hospital. As a result, cars panicked him and he was not able to pass his driving test until he could face the ghost of his father's scary driving. When he realized as an adult that he could choose to be a safe driver, he drove with an understanding friend until he overcame his fears. He was no longer a helpless passenger in someone else's car.

How Our Earliest Ghosts Are Formed

Our beliefs about what the world is like are largely in place by the time we are three years of age. If we feel safe and loved and we are well nourished, then we will likely believe the world is a secure, friendly, abundant place. If these early years are filled with loss, pain, hunger, or violence, then we will likely see the world as a scary, hostile, overwhelming place. Not only our child-rearing styles but also our politics and religious beliefs can be affected by our early experiences. For example, a man whose mother died in childbirth with him felt shunned by his father and stepmother. As an adult he turned to a highly paternalistic and rigid religion for personal security and as a substitute family.

Childhood Experiences Can Dictate
Adult Beliefs and Behaviors

If we want to avoid the traps set by our ghosts, we must understand how our childhood experiences affect our adult beliefs and behaviors. Otherwise, outdated fears and ideas will persist in our minds as if we were still little children. Experiences we don't even remember can determine what we feel and what we do. It's like trying to drive somewhere using maps that are 20, 30, or even 150 years out of date.

Ghosts that come between our children and us are often images of our parents as we saw them when we were our children's ages. Have you ever heard yourself say something in anger to your child that sounds like what your parents said to you? Many of us have caught ourselves doing that because memories of the family we grew up in become the patterns we use to construct our own families. Faulty patterns—based on life in a troubled family—lead us to form faulty new family relationships. For example, a surprising number of my patients grew up with an absent parent and went on to become absent parents or to marry spouses who left when the children were little. These patients' childhood experiences led them to expect that a family will always have an absent parent.

Ghosts by Nature Are Tricky

When ghosts stand between another person and us, they can make us believe that the person we see in front of us is really someone else. This tricks us into acting as if the current relationship is the same as one from the past. A man in his middle twenties had been through a dozen failed relationships looking for his high-school sweetheart. Each time, the woman left him after realizing he would never stop wishing that she were this other woman.

Ghosts make us confuse people in our lives today with people from our past. For example, it's not your fault that you remind me of the girl next door who seemed to delight in hurting my feelings when I was nine years old, and it shouldn't be your problem. But if I don't recognize her ghost in our relationship now, you will be dealing with my wariness and anger, even though you have been entirely decent to me. It will be my problem to solve, although you could gently remind me that there seems to be an unfinished relationship between the two of us.

An Experiment to Demonstrate How Ghosts Intrude on Us

Set up a slide projector and project a life-size image of someone onto a wall. Now ask someone else to step in front of the picture so that the face from the slide is on the live person's face. Whose face do you see? The slide image represents the ghost of someone from the past. Our minds do this to us all the time. The more clearly we recognize that this is happening, the more easily we can remember that there is a living person right in front of us who is different from the one whose picture we are projecting. Sometimes parents have trouble seeing the independent young man or woman who really exists because they see only the ghost of their dependent little child.

Now redirect the projection so you see it clearly and separately from the person in front of you. Then turn off the projector, both the mechanical one and the one in your mind. The latter can be hard to turn off. Despite our best efforts, old feelings may persist. In that case, we have to get rid of these old feelings by remembering them in all their intensity and finding a way to accept that what happened is now over.

SUGGESTIONS FOR CHANGE. Write down your feelings toward people from the past with whom you still have conflicts. Sharing stories with a sympathetic listener, especially someone with similar experiences, can help, as long as the focus is on making constructive decisions rather than complaining together. The self-help sections of many bookstores contain excellent workbooks that provide guided exercises in clarifying feelings, reframing them, and practicing new habits of thought that create hopeful options for effective action (see appendix D).

For scars too deep to heal through writing about them or talking with a sympathetic friend or for people who simply work better with the help of a coach, working with a professional psychotherapist may be the most effective solution.

Tracking Ghosts

Ghosts are potentially everywhere in our lives. Keeping them from intruding on us can be a real challenge. Here are four questions to help you locate your ghosts so you can learn to handle them.

- In what ways do these bad feelings seem familiar?
- Who are the people that these feelings make me remember?
- How far back and in what circumstances do I remember feeling like this?
- How old do I feel when I'm feeling this way?

Common Ghosts

The easiest ghosts to recognize may be those that recreate in our heads the very words and emotions we heard and felt from our parents—Mother's bad temper or Father's icy threats, for example. These memories are aroused when our child does something that reminds us of an experience from our own childhood. More subtle ghosts arrive simply as beliefs we take for granted or feelings we have for no reason—fears overwhelming us out of the blue, self-criticism, or persistent feelings that we are worthless, ugly, invincible, better than others, inadequate, or unlovable.

Remarkably, parts of our minds remain untainted by ghosts from our past and are able to see the truth. Deep down we know when we have been deceived by false images. Cherish this ability to see the truth and have faith in the power of the human spirit. From watching the incredible courage of my patients, I have come to believe that the human spirit, which we all share, is amazingly tough.

In *A Christmas Carol,* Charles Dickens's Scrooge faces ghosts in his dreams. But his stinginess was probably caused by the kind of ghosts we're discussing here—legacies from his past. We are never told who modeled such selfishness during his childhood, but no doubt their voices were strong in his head while he went about his miserly business. (Perhaps he was raised in a cold and neglectful orphanage by caregivers who mostly hated children.) The spirits of Christmas come to awaken him to new truths about himself and to liberate him from his personal ghosts.

Occasionally ghosts dare us to recognize them. Paula Durren, whom we will meet shortly, shared an example. When he was five, Paula's son Jeremy would slouch on their sofa. His innocent behavior made her feel like screaming at him. It took her several months to remember that when she was five, her father developed an ulcer and would retreat to the sofa in pain and wouldn't let anybody comfort him. She was baffled that such a powerful memory took so long to surface, but when it did, she recalled the time, like it was yesterday, that an ambulance came to the house to take her father to the hospital. She believed she would never see him again. This recollection startled her, but she was relieved to remember after so many years. Once she understood the ghost that had caused her reaction, her son's slouching ceased to panic her.

THE DURREN FAMILY'S STORY

Paula and Germaine Durren married soon after graduating from college. Germaine completed a master's degree in architecture and accepted an apprenticeship in a small architectural firm. Jeremy was born during Paula's third year of medical school. Tawnia arrived during Paula's second year as a family medicine resident. Both children were thriving and doing well in school when I met them. The Durrens requested professional counseling for the first time in their lives after Jeremy at age fifteen got caught shoplifting at a local drugstore.

Jeremy's plan had been to pick up some free condoms with his friends. Instead he faced store security, $250 in fines, and a trip to juvenile court. When I met them, his parents were so upset I thought Jeremy had shot somebody. "How do we make sense of all this?" "Has he become a thief?" "What's he doing stealing condoms?" "Have we failed him?" "What did we do wrong?"

Germaine told me he had sometimes wanted to slap his son black-and-blue. From the boy's dejection, I assumed he had already been sharply reprimanded. Jeremy's action had upset Paula well beyond what she thought was appropriate for the shoplifting alone. She was shaken and unsure. Twelve-year-old Tawnia seemed pleased her brother was in trouble, but she was angry with him for getting her mother so upset.

Germaine: *(to Jeremy)* When I remember my father, I think of an angry doberman. I still hear him in my head. "Come here, son, you've got a lesson to learn." It seemed like he was always finding some excuse to smack me. That's what's so scary right now. There's a part of me that feels like smacking you. I promise you I won't, but the feeling is real strong. There have been times I wasn't sure I could stop myself.

The next time we met, Paula and Germaine reported several days of arguing and long periods of silence. Germaine was clearly frustrated.

Germaine: Paula, I can't take any more of this tension. Either we talk with each other or I've got to go someplace.

Paula: You're the one who wanted to beat your son.

Germaine: You're right. That's what I felt like doing!

Paula: You will never lay a hand on any child of mine! I don't feel like I even know you.

Germaine: I am trying to tell you how furious I am so I won't hurt him. I am doing my best to cool down. I'm talking to you so I won't do something stupid.

Paula and Germaine got sidetracked by ghost messages from Germaine's past with his father, but they kept listening to each other.

Germaine saw himself get boiling mad like he remembered his father used to do. Fortunately, he caught himself and called for help. Jeremy hadn't been planning to defy his parents. He just got caught up in an impulse with friends. The $250 fine for shoplifting surprised him.

Germaine's stopping his own overreaction was a crucial first step in preventing more injuries from this incident. He felt the impact of ghosts that had remained mostly dormant since his own teenage experiments with independence. He controlled the voice and fury of his own father in his head, rather than letting it control him. He saw that his rage was out of proportion to Jeremy's misdeed.

SUGGESTIONS FOR CHANGE. Write a list of your childhood misfortunes. Then write brief answers to the following questions:

- How powerful or intrusive are your memories?
- Are you reluctant to think about any of them?
- What feelings do you get now when you think about what happened?
- How does each event affect your life today?

Caution: Major traumas may feel "too hot to handle." Don't push yourself beyond what feels manageable. If panic arises, back off. Overwhelming yourself again is not helpful. Spend a little bit of time remembering, then pause and make sure you can stop worrying. The key to trauma recovery is to remain in control of

> your emotions this time around, not to make yourself a victim
> again of excessive fear.

The Leaky Foundation

Frightening childhood experiences create in our adult lives a leaky
foundation that is more readily flooded by current storms. Children
who face loneliness, fear, or shame early in life will find it harder to
cope with trouble as adults, especially if they are not taught how to
feel safe during new events.

Once we see the leaks, we can begin to fix them. Each of us has the
ability to love and to forgive others and ourselves. Children inevitably
remind us of our own childhoods, so it's also inevitable that the crises
of raising our children will be made worse by ghosts or legacies from
our own childhood experiences.

The Durren Family's Ghosts

The surprise of Jeremy's shoplifting submerged his parents in memories of events from before Jeremy was born and for which Jeremy
clearly had no responsibility. These memories threatened to impose
outmoded choices onto the present situation. Jeremy reminded
Germaine of himself as an adventurous teenager, and he reminded
Paula of how self-conscious she could be.

Germaine: Man, if I ever pulled something like this and my dad
found out, I don't know for sure what he would have
done, but it would have hurt me. There were times
when my friends and I would go looking for thrills and
we just prayed he never found out.

Jeremy: Yeah? What kind of thrills?

Germaine: *(to me)* Should we be talking about this? *(I nodded.)* Okay. One time my friend Ron and me took the keys to his sister's car and ended up driving it into a ditch. His mom was so frustrated with us she cried. His sister slugged him, but they never did tell my parents. I think we were fourteen or fifteen at the time.

Jeremy: If you did stuff like that, why are you guys so upset about what I did?

Germaine: That's a fair question. One answer is, you got caught, so I know about it.

Paula: *(to Jeremy)* I realized I was a whole lot madder and more frightened than it made sense to be over a few condoms. Talking about it since you were caught has made things clearer to me. I was really embarrassed when I heard you were arrested. My first thought was, "How am I going to tell your grandmother?" Then I worried about what they were going to think at work. "Dr. Durren can't even take care of her own kid." I felt like I was back in school, afraid to bring my friends home. I didn't want to be seen by anyone.

Jeremy: Mom, I'm sorry about all this. I wasn't trying to hurt you.

Paula: I know you weren't. You weren't even thinking about us. But you don't get off so easily. It astonishes me that you would steal condoms! *(Jeremy blushed.)* And we are definitely going to talk about what you planned to do with them. Maybe this is enough for now. I feel better now that I've been able to talk about this.

Emancipation or Emotional Warfare

Paula and Germaine, like all parents, face a dilemma: either we trust our children and let them grow up or we live with tension and arguments. In family battles for control, too often everybody loses. To quote an anonymous sage, "The art of parenting teenagers is the art of losing gracefully." Our job as parents is to let go by the time our teenagers are ready to assume control of their own lives. Their rage, turned outward into defiance or inward into depression, will be our reward for too much parental control.

Excessive Parental Control

Risks of emotional and physical injury rise steeply whenever parents exercise excessive control over their children. Good parenting provides safety for both children and parents. Too much control serves the short-term comfort of parents at the expense of their children's long-term character development. When the real goal of my parental decisions is to relieve my own anxieties, rather than to provide for my children's healthy development, I run a high risk of using too much control.

Consider these statements: "You will do what I say and do it right now," "I know what is best for you," and "You will not talk to me (embarrass me/anger me) that way." Any one of these statements might be heard from a good parent in good form. They become excessive when a parent continually ignores what the child needs and wants. Good parenting is educational and encouraging, and every situation is a teaching opportunity. Every time we interact with our children, they learn by example. Occasionally, they allow us to teach them by instruction. When the goal is helping children to mature and to find happiness, every interaction teaches or reinforces a lesson.

SUGGESTIONS FOR CHANGE. On a bad day, when you don't really have energy or patience to teach a lesson in good behavior, show your children by example how they can deal with their own bad days. Be gracious and admit your own grumpiness. When you make a mistake, say so honestly. Ask your children's forgiveness and mean it. If you ask them to make a special effort for you in these moments—being especially quiet, for example—make it a good lesson by clearly admitting that the problem is your own exhaustion, you do not blame them, and you genuinely appreciate their help.

Our children can handle our being out of commission at times. What they cannot handle is uncertainty about our love and their safety during our worst moods. If our children come to believe we will sometimes hurt their dignity, even if it is only when we are out of sorts, then they will live in fear of our bad moods. Their belief that we will criticize them or ignore their ideas will push them toward rebellion and depression.

Sooner or later, without love and humor, these family frictions can build. When we're afraid to see our own contributions to the conflicts or afraid to change, the miscommunication and hurt feelings in the family only get worse.

Telling the Truth Will Defuse Our Ghosts

Building trust within our families starts with telling the truth. Our children learn honesty from us. Even with very little children we can convey the importance of being honest by the ways we demonstrate our own commitment to telling the truth. By facing up to our own ghosts, we let the truth gain control of our decision making.

Sometimes in family therapy, the children are ready to open up and tell the truth about the family but the parents are not. One father told me he planned to talk with his daughter about the problems she had revealed in one of our sessions. He lied to me. Instead, he went home and yelled at her for being ungrateful and lazy. He was punishing her for telling truths about the family that he was not ready to consider because they made him so uncomfortable. When parents are preoccupied with looking good no matter what, children suffer. If parents hide the truth about the family, their children will have trouble figuring out what the truth really is.

DEALING WITH DAY-TO-DAY STRESS

Ghost legacies by their nature add stress to your daily life (which no doubt is already stressful enough) and make it even more important that you *take good care of yourself— physically, emotionally, and spiritually.*

Conserve your energy by using it only in ways that make your life better. This means making good choices. What will make the tasks you have to do (such as changing diapers, fixing meals, cleaning house, or going to work) more enjoyable and relaxing? And what energy are you wasting on criticizing yourself or complaining about a messy house? The key to taking good care of yourself is to find ways to celebrate your life, whatever your situation. Sing a song or play music that awakens your heart. Arrange for someone else to watch your children so you have regular time to yourself. Meditate on loving your family members and yourself. Notice the life and beauty around you. Borrow energy from the birds and the wind as well as other people to fuel the changes you decide to make. The only healthy way to deal with helplessness is to develop a plan of action—the more full of life the better.

IDENTIFYING THE ROOTS OF FAMILY CONFLICT— QUESTIONS TO ASK

Here are more questions to help you identify the ways in which the roots of family conflict affect your family. Keep your answers for future reference.

- What situations recurrently frustrate you?
- In what ways do these conflicts remind you of earlier conflicts in your life?
- Who from the past do current family members in conflict remind you of?
- In what situations do you feel exhausted, irritable, ashamed, angry, or anxious?
- Are you overusing alcohol or other drugs, food, tobacco, or caffeine?
- When are you likely to put a negative slant on events?

Once you identify the roots of a particular conflict, it's time to find new ways to handle it.

- How can you best keep past problems in the past?
- What helps you reliably learn from your mistakes?

Find someone you can talk with about your answers to these questions. It is more productive to discuss these issues with someone you like, you trust, and who cares about you than it is to fret over them alone. Review the information about mental disorders in appendix B. Share with a friend your fears and hopes. Read this book together or try one of the suggested readings in appendix D. Keep a journal. If you don't have someone to share these ideas with, set a goal to find a new friend or locate a counselor.

STEP 3

PUT YOUR OWN LIFE
IN ORDER FIRST

Find the courage to start fixing whatever is

broken within yourself first, then you can

effectively help your family.

HEALING YOUR FAMILY starts with healing yourself. The biggest mistake I see parents make is to model the very behaviors they want their children to stop.

You can't teach your children to cooperate by forcing them with threats or intimidation. Yelling at your kids to stop yelling won't set the example you want. They learn from what you do. Remember the saying "Your behavior speaks so loudly I can't hear a word you are saying."

In Step 3 the focus is on healing yourself and developing the skills you need to accomplish the goals you have set for your family. You are the most powerful tool for change in your family—you can model the way you want people to treat each other, and you can lead your family in working for changes that you convince them are possible. These will not be easy tasks. The next three chapters will help you to prepare for the challenges ahead. Chapter 7 will show you how to look at your own behaviors and begin to act in ways that promote cooperative family interactions. Chapter 8 will help you brush up on your parenting skills. And chapter 9 will assist you in clarifying your parenting goals so your energy can be directed toward the outcomes you really want.

Chapter 7

HEAL THYSELF

Messages full of criticism or anger draw down your children's reserves of love and respect, so use them sparingly. Instead, send messages of love and encouragement with ideas for better ways they can have fun and find the self-esteem they need.

Instead of saying, "Stop that!" try addressing your child by name and saying "[your child's name], that annoys me when you do that. Now please do [name something acceptable] instead." Or simply say, "You seem to need something from me right now. What is it?"

When your child is annoying you, intervene before you get too upset. That way you're more likely to stay calm and encouraging. If you are already angry or exasperated, you have waited too long to direct your child toward more acceptable activity.

If you find yourself already angry, be especially careful to let your child know what you want her to do.

- "Sit quietly for three minutes, and then I can take you to the store."
- "Do your best for the next ten minutes to clean up your room by yourself, and then I will come and help."
- "You want my attention right now, don't you? What do you need that can't wait?"

When you recognize ways in which your own tone and behavior aggravate your children, you have already begun to heal your family.

Negative, irritable, sarcastic comments on your part will always invite the same in return from your children. You will create change in your children's behavior most quickly when you replace your own frustration at not getting what you want from them with patient encouragement of what you do want. The edict to physicians holds for parents, too: heal thyself. When you improve your own behavior first, you can make a fair demand that other family members improve their behavior, too.

My dad used to kid me when he made a mistake by telling me to "Do as I say, not as I do." Fortunately for me, my dad's mistakes were usually minor ones that I could easily forgive because I knew absolutely that he loved me and wanted what was best for me. His infrequent major mistakes were always corrected once he saw them, amends were genuine, and the mistakes were not repeated.

Mistakes Are Acceptable, Unless You Repeat Them

I have yet to meet a family with chronic problems where the parents did not repeatedly make the problems worse. So your first assignment is to stop repeating your mistakes. Just stop. Don't do it anymore. You've probably said "Stop it!" to your children many times. Now it's your turn.

No matter how hard it may be, that's your assignment. Find any way that works to bring your own behaviors under control so you're no longer a source of irritation. Here are a few ideas: Instead of nagging, make your request once. Make it clear you mean what you say by following up with real consequences for compliance or noncompliance. Instead of criticizing, say what you want in place of pointing out the behavior you don't like. Instead of complaining, offer an alternative. Do something that changes what your children do in response to you. If their responses become more cooperative, keep doing what you're doing. If not, change what you do. Keep trying new ideas until your interactions with them feel affirming and productive for you and them. If whatever you try makes the problem worse, try not responding at all next time. Once you successfully break the habit of arguing, you'll be ready to develop skills and strategies that will help your family heal.

Of course, external circumstances can create enormous stresses for families. However, I know several refugee families who lost homes and loved ones and still maintained love, respect, and humor among themselves and with others. Steady, loving, and respectful approaches that spring from true self-respect create an atmosphere of happiness, love, and understanding in which children will thrive. When you overreact, lose your temper, criticize too harshly, or demean your child, catch yourself. Acknowledge the mistake. And don't let yourself make that mistake again. (Make a different one next time and make it a loving one.) That way your apologies can be genuine, and eventually you will learn what works the first time to create a win-win solution rather than having to make yet another new mistake.

As parents, we teach our most lasting lessons by what we do. The more consistently we model the attitudes and actions we want from our children, the more likely they will follow our examples. Unfortunately, when we model insults or sarcasm or irritability, they quickly respond with rudeness of their own. This sequence is our responsibility to change, both because we started it and because we are the ones in charge.

Healing starts with us.

SUGGESTIONS FOR CHANGE. Keep in mind that our goal is to raise healthy, self-confident, and caring children. Does your own behavior support or undermine that goal? Tape record yourself directing your children the way you usually do. Put it away for a week, and then listen to it. How do you sound? Does the tone of what you said fit with the results you wanted? Would you really like someone else to speak to you with the tone and words you used? Did you include love and humor? Did your words help your children to feel better about themselves?

If any of your answers were no, rehearse different ways you might deal with a similar situation next time. For example, if your tone of voice seemed to irritate your child, tape record yourself using a tone that is soothing and reassuring and see if you feel different when you hear yourself. Remember that seeing the humor in a situation will help you to keep your composure and to think more creatively about ways to meet everyone's basic needs.

Chapter 8

FIVE BASIC SKILLS OF
GOOD PARENTING

In this chapter I outline the basic skills I believe are at the core of good parenting. So much of what we do as parents depends on maintaining a good attitude. If we can find ways to stay loving, firm, good-natured, and creative, our children will be happier and more cooperative with us.

To be a consistently good parent you need to develop these five core skills:

1. Talk lovingly to your infants and listen lovingly to your children

2. See through your children's eyes

3. Model love and respect

4. Do what your parental heart of hearts tells you is right

5. Persevere and enjoy your children

Basic Skill #1: Talk Lovingly to Your Infants and Listen Lovingly to Your Children

Communicate your love in everything you say and do. Your children are precious and will bring you many of life's greatest joys if you always treasure them. From the day your baby arrives, talk lovingly to her. Sing and tell her with beautiful sounds how wonderful she is and how much hope you hold for her future. Accept the strain and exhaustion of raising her as part of your decision to become a parent.

Give your child words to express her feelings, whatever they are. Ask, "Are you hungry?" "Are you tired?" "Do your teeth hurt?" Say, "You seem excited." "I think you're sad." And always let her know she is beautiful and precious and you love her. You will never spoil a child by loving him or her too much.

Read to your child. Play music that soothes both of you. And let her hear you talk lovingly and respectfully with your partner and neighbors. By watching you she is learning how to soothe herself and talk with other people.

When your second baby arrives, your love becomes a duet. Use the same affirmations for the new baby and add reassurances for your firstborn: "You are precious and your new brother is precious, too. Mommy and Daddy's hearts are very big. There is room to love many people, and you will always be special just for being you." This begins your first child's introduction to a shared world where there is love enough for each and every child.

As your children learn to use language by listening to you, shift your focus to listening to them. Ask questions that encourage their curiosity. Help them learn the words that give them access to new information and provide them a way to tell what they need. As your children grow older, reward their eagerness to share with you by listening patiently without interruptions.

Children who love to talk with you will be easy to direct toward positive behavior. Your act of listening closely is powerfully affirming to a child's sense of self. Children who like themselves and who know their parents like them cooperate more readily both because they like to please parents who make them feel good and because they have less reason to rebel. The earlier and more consistently you reinforce their communicating with you spontaneously, the more avenues will be open to you to teach them how to get along well with other people.

When your children know you are interested in what they have to say, their curiosity and desire to please you become your allies. Raise interesting questions that will help them to discover the truths you want them to know:

"You two want to play with the same doll. How might you share?"

"How do you think she felt when you told her girls can't play foursquare?"

"Is there a different way you'd like to study for your next test?"

"What did you learn by getting so drunk last night?"

SUGGESTIONS FOR CHANGE. Listening lets you enjoy your children's developing minds. Keep a journal of their wisdom and memorable remarks. Ever hear ones like these two?

"Mom, was I ever a hamster?"

"I don't like it. What is it?"

Basic Skill #2: See through Your Children's Eyes

If you see conflicts as your children see them, you will not only nurture their souls with your solutions, you will model behavior that will become the backbone of their social graces. Your effort to know their feelings sets the example for them to value what others say and feel. You will also see yourself more clearly and be more likely to catch your own mistakes. Children will be honest unless they learn honesty doesn't work or, worse, that it backfires. Praise them for telling the truth as they see it. That way you can understand their perspectives and they can learn from their mistakes. This also teaches them to accept responsibility for the decisions they make.

Let each conflict be a chance to learn how your child thinks. Question them to expand your own understanding and theirs.

Daughter:	I had to clean up after the dog last week. It's Seth's turn.
Mother:	Seth has a term paper due on Friday. I'll get him to take your turn next week.
Daughter:	But he always gets out of doing it.
Mother:	Tell me what you're upset about.
Daughter:	Dog poop is gross. Besides, she's Seth's dog, not mine.
Mother:	You mean she's not your dog, too.
Daughter:	I don't want her to be my dog anymore.
Mother:	Taking care of a poopy dog isn't much fun, is it?
Daughter:	No!
Mother:	So you'd rather not have a dog at all?
Daughter:	Well, I like her to play with sometimes.
Mother:	Someone has to clean up after her. She can't do it herself.
Daughter:	Yeah, but why me?
Mother:	Let's do it together this time. It's all part of having a dog. It's like having a baby in the house.
Daughter:	I don't think I want any babies!

When we have our children's attention, we can use these moments to teach important lessons. The immediate issue above is cleaning up after the dog, but the bigger issue is responsibility for other living creatures, including babies.

Basic Skill #3: Model Love and Respect

Flip Wilson was a very funny man who created a female comedy character named Geraldine, whose favorite line was "What you see is what you get!" Keep in mind that what your children see you do is what you're likely to get back from them. Treat them with dignity from the very start and they will treat you with dignity for the rest of your life.

Our children observe and experience how we treat them and each other. They absorb our attitudes and ways of relating and make them their own. When they watch us routinely belittle each other or criticize every little detail, they learn that's how they should behave. They soak up our examples to replay them back to us and to other children.

Model love and respect since these are what we truly want from our children. We parents must always operate by the Golden Rule—when our children are around and also at times we think they're not watching. I know too many parents whose bad behavior away from home was somehow reported back to their children, undermining the parents' credibility, or parents who lost their composure at home and slipped into behaviors they more commonly practiced away from home. Even if you're consistently loving and respectful, your children will need specific guidance from you from time to time.

Father: I hear you shoved a boy at school today.

Son: He hit me.

Father: What happened before that?

Son: I was playing with another friend and he just came over and hit me.

Father: What do you think he really wanted?

Son: I don't know.

Father: Why did he choose to hit you?

Son: I don't know.

Father: How about you try to talk with him?

Son: He says mean things to me.

Father: Maybe he wants to be your friend but doesn't know how to ask.

Son: Really?

Father: Next time you see him, ask him to play with you and your friend and see what happens.

Basic Skill #4: Do What Your Heart of Hearts Tells You Is Right

We all have to answer to the mirror. When you look at yourself in the morning, do you like the person you see? Are you happy with the parenting decisions you have made recently? Deep down you have to believe in what you do as a parent or you and your children will crash into a very painful wall of misunderstanding. It's important to be loving and respectful because love and respect wear better on our consciences than irritability, complaining, or intimidation.

Try guiding your children, rather than forcing them to obey you. Lead them where you want them to go, rather than force them. Think of discipline as education.

- "You need to leave for your school bus in ten minutes. It looks like you're having trouble deciding on what shirt to wear. Which of these three will be most comfortable on a warm day like today?"
- "Give me a hand with the garbage, will you?"
- "It's not my turn to wash the dishes either, but let's do them together and get it out of the way."
- "Do you need help with your homework tonight?"
- "You can be as rude as you want to be, but I won't be much help until you tell me clearly what you want me to do."

Children who are taught and supported through caring and respectful relationships rarely require punishment. They are treated with respect and affection and thereby learn to treat others the same way. Time-outs for misbehavior become opportunities to calm down and think about a conflict in new ways. Our intent in disciplining our children is to help them see their problems in creative and helpful ways, not to make them feel guilty or diminished.

The toughest challenges for many parents arrive with puberty. Our teenagers flex the character strength we nurtured in them, and suddenly we face formidable opponents. Celebrate the ways they challenge you, even if what they do hurts your feelings or makes you angry, and redirect their negative energy and your own by complimenting them on their strength, creativity, and courage to stand up to you. If they test your anger, don't take the bait. When their confrontations exceed your true limits, set consequences that enforce mutual safety and dignity.

Sean just couldn't stay out of his parents' wet bar. He would sneak vodka, bourbon, wine, or beer—whatever he found in stock. He tried concealing his thefts by adding water to fill up the bottles. When the liquor became so diluted his mother noticed, she started making public comments about how someone had cut into their liquor supply. Sean's mom knew pretty well whom to suspect, but chose not to make a scene. Instead, she took Sean aside and congratulated him on how clever he was, asked which form of alcohol he liked best, and asked him what he knew about the family's history of alcohol abuse. She also asked him if he needed his parents to remove all alcohol from the home. He said he thought that was a good idea. When she told Sean's father the plan, he objected at first and said it was his house. On reflection, however, he agreed that they wanted to set a good example for Sean. So the alcohol was removed and Sean felt lucky his mom understood.

Enforce the rules that your parental heart of hearts says you must enforce, and find ways to accept the challenges to your authority that validate your teenager's budding independence. If your teenager refuses to clean his room, find a way to ignore it; if you need to intervene, tell him it's to uphold the rights of other family members rather than to tell him what to do. Practicing patience with your teenager can strengthen your soul. You are lifting yourself above your exasperation.

The more you practice patience and good humor with your teen, the stronger you'll get in withstanding his or her seemingly inborn need to impersonate a monster. You may spend years in the trenches, but this stage in your teenager's life will also pass.

In the case of Germaine and Paula, when they saw that no real harm was done, they were able to defuse their anger at Jeremy's experiment with shoplifting. They saved themselves from a nasty and fruitless family storm. In the end they laughed together, Jeremy took some heavy teasing, and they grew stronger as a family.

SUGGESTIONS FOR CHANGE. Here's a chance to consciously choose your own style of parenting. Reflect on the last really tense encounter with one of your children. You will discover as you look at fights that break out between you and your children that you have a number of choices that will either increase the tension and escalate the confrontation or decrease the tension and lead toward peaceful coexistence, if not loving harmony.

- How was the very first spark of tension introduced this time? What set the tension off in you? Were you already frustrated when your child showed up? If so, what were you so tense about? If not, what about your child's entrance set you off?

- Once the tension was present, what did you do to reverse it? Or did you add to it? If you added to it, where did your reaction come from and what might you have done differently to reverse the tension instead? Here's a good chance to rehearse in your head how you will keep yourself calm and stay in charge of the tension next time. If you don't fall into the trap your child lays for

---

you or you lay for yourself (the hole in the sidewalk), you have a
chance to calm your tensions and those of your child and work
out an acceptable solution for both of you.

Basic Skill #5: Persevere and Enjoy Your Children

You've accepted by now that parenting is difficult. No matter why you
chose to jump into the storm-tossed ocean of parenthood, you're in
it now. As you accept where you are and learn how to navigate in this
difficult environment, you'll get stronger and more comfortable in
the role you chose.

Learn to conserve your energy by picking your fights carefully.
Otherwise, relax. You're in a marathon. You don't want to keep sprint-
ing off like a dog after squirrels. You'll wear yourself out. Instead,
soothe yourself and your children with music, reading a story, or
a walk in the park. Strike up conversations with them about the
world around you. Listen to their enthusiasm and curiosity. Make
up stories that excite their imaginations. Tell your children about
your own childhood and what your parents were like. And always
reward their inventiveness and perseverance with your undivided
attention.

Sometimes just trying to make the best of a difficult situation
becomes a special family moment. One sloppy, rainy weekend my
wife and I and our seven- and ten-year-old sons were housebound by
the weather, so we huddled together around a heater and took turns
reading *Third Man on the Mountain*.[13] I think we also shared hot
soup. The book carried us away for the entire afternoon into a world
of mountains, adventure, and a young man coming of age.

Sharing family time together creates the atmosphere of happiness,
love, and understanding that is our goal. Each small success launches

the next. Steady good humor and steady commitment to doing things together makes and maintains the peace at home.

Every chance you get, enjoy your children's cooperation and independence. As you need to, reign them in for their moral, emotional, and physical safety. Otherwise, savor their explorations of family, friendships, and self-sufficiency.

For children, giving parents a hard time is like aerobics for their growing souls. The personal strength they exercise by pushing you around is the strength that will propel and protect them in the wider, less loving world. Reinforce it and compliment them for it, while at the same time you insist on some approximation of love and respect in return. If your sense of humor goes flat, take a break and recharge your batteries, with outside help if needed.

SUGGESTIONS FOR CHANGE. Possibly the hardest part about change is the perseverance required. Take a few minutes to meditate on the time and effort it took you to accomplish some of the things you are most proud of. What was your most hard-won success? How long did it take you? How long did it take you to get through school? How about learning a new job or successfully courting your partner? Have you ever broken a longstanding bad habit like lying or being late? How much effort did it take you?

Changing old patterns in your family that lead to recurrent pain may well be as demanding as any of your other major accomplishments. Keep your eye on the prize and don't give up easily. Generosity and patient good humor when combined with unflappable commitment to safe and loving boundaries will create the atmosphere of happiness, love, and understanding we are working toward. When you mean "no," say so clearly, calmly, and with a firmness your children will not mistake for uncertainty. And tell them what you *do* want them to do instead. That way they can feel secure in your commitment to their long-range well-being.

Chapter 9

REACHING YOUR GOALS

The United Nations (UN) Convention on the Rights of the Child, now signed by 202 of the 203 countries in the UN,[14] is the most widely endorsed document in human history. It brings us a nearly universal consensus on healthy child rearing. The preamble states,

> Childhood is entitled to special care and assistance . . . the child, for the full and harmonious development of his or her personality, should grow up in a family environment, in an atmosphere of happiness, love and understanding; the child should be fully prepared to live an individual life in society, and brought up in the spirit of the ideals proclaimed in the Charter of the United Nations, and in particular in the spirit of peace, dignity, tolerance, freedom, equality and solidarity.[15]

This global agreement sets the stage for us to create our own healthy family environment. We frame our goals with two questions:

- What kind of people do we want our children to become?
- How can we be good models for our children now?

Practice of the virtues listed below supports a family atmosphere of happiness, love, and understanding and helps our children to find meaning and satisfaction in their lives, especially as the world becomes more complex, competitive, and heartless. These are virtues that permeate the parenting styles and child interactions in healthy families. They need to be woven into our goals and developed as parenting skills. It's always helpful to observe ourselves from time to time to see how well we practice what we want from our children. Here's my core list:

- honesty
- gentleness
- assertiveness
- self-discipline
- tenacity
- mutual caring
- celebration
- humor

You may well find as you reflect on these virtues that their absence highlights problems that subvert the effectiveness of your parenting.

Loving and Respecting Your Children

Loving and respecting each other is the *goal* as well as the *means* for healing our families. It is the only sure way to get our children's lasting cooperation, obedience, and love. When discipline satisfies a need for parental power before serving the well-being of children, the table is set for lifelong pain. If you want your children to obey you, frame your demands so that obeying you strengthens their self-esteem.

Keep Your Initial Goals Simple

Piecing personal and family goals together is similar to doing a jigsaw puzzle. There's the big picture—how we want our overall life to unfold—and also the realities we have to face day by day. Keep things simple so you don't overwhelm yourself. Start with what's right in front of you. What is your goal for today? Given the day ahead of you, what would make it worthwhile? What would give you a sense of accomplishment if you did it today?

> **SUGGESTIONS FOR CHANGE.** Make a brief list of your goals for today. Number them in order of importance. Do this daily for a week. Record what you accomplish and how you feel about yourself at the end of each day. After you get better at reaching each day's goals, you can plan further into the future.

Margaret Hazen's unstable moods created a lifelong pattern of disorganized and self-defeating behavior. Her medicines subdued her excessive moodiness but did not change her habits. She still needed to work on setting goals and defining her problems in ways that clarified what to do to make her situation better.

Margaret: Dr. Hall, I want to get my life back. But look at me. My hair's a mess. My house is a mess. My kids are a mess. My whole life's a mess. I think I must be wasting your time. *(She rose to leave.)*

Dr. Hall: Margaret, you're not wasting my time. Your life is out of control. That's why you're here. Right?

Margaret: Right.

Dr. Hall: So be gentle with yourself. Break the problem into smaller pieces so it is clearer what to do. What one task would you like to accomplish within the next week?

Margaret: I've been wanting to get my hair done for a month now. I even had an appointment, but the baby got sick and I'm broke again. Okay, I could clean my bedroom. It's a sty. There are clothes all over the floor and papers falling off my desk. I can't remember what clothes are clean and what are not, so I put them all back in the laundry and wash them again. Some of my clothes get washed three or four times before I wear them again. I could do that.

Margaret settled on cleaning her bedroom, and it became clear she had a very hard time keeping herself focused. We worked together to adjust her medicine doses and to set specific, reachable goals so at the end of each day she would know what she had accomplished.

At first she had difficulty defining clear goals, but she persisted. She said she wanted to be a better mother, so I asked her what she would do to be a better mother today. She wanted her house clean, so I got her to break the whole job into blocks of work she knew she could do. In time she became quite skilled in naming specific tasks and specific actions she would do. She learned to evaluate her actions as to how well they worked and how she felt about herself doing them. As her skills improved, she was able to set specific daily tasks for herself. She got her hair done with money budgeted from her next paycheck. And she put away her laundry, which reduced her laundry loads by half. Her next goal was to elicit more cooperation from her children.

Margaret: I was seeing these things as just a series of endless tasks that I couldn't get done. I felt like I was on a treadmill. It really helps to think of them as small ways I can feel good about myself—little steps to get my confidence back.

Guarantee Success

To be effective, short-term goals should be designed such that success is guaranteed. If we carefully choose tasks within our ability and resources, then with self-discipline we can carry them out. If our self-discipline is weak, then strengthened self-discipline is an important goal.

If you can induce yourself to clean out the garage with the reward of going out for ice cream, then you know your problem with cleaning the garage is pretty straightforward—you just need a little motivation. If you can't get it done even with your three best friends helping, then you are facing more formidable obstacles, such as poorly defined priorities, conflicts about cleaning up (ghosts), or problems with focus and organization that might need professional evaluation.

One helpful way to grasp these issues is to write down your own basic goals for parenting. Start with the big picture first so you have a framework within which to make your day-to-day choices. What are the real reasons you want to be a parent? What kind of life do you want for yourself, for your spouse or your partner, and for your children? Your answers to these questions become your goals for parenting. Later you can break these goals into smaller, workable tasks you actually plan to do each day.

Sample Goals and Values

Good parenting needs clear goals and a plan. Here, as a model, are the goals and values my wife and I relied on to raise our two sons.

We want our children

- To be vital human beings, fully alive, and able to engage the abundance of life around them

- To respect, enjoy, and care about themselves, each other, their parents, the human community, and the living planet that sustains us all
- To know genuinely how to protect themselves and their world from harm and to act strongly on their knowledge
- To face themselves honestly
- To find their own competence and self-confidence
- To be determined and curious
- To share love throughout their lives
- In short, to know happiness, harmony, and true fulfillment in their lives and to include their parents in some of it

And here is the pledge we made to them:

We pledge to our children our tenacious love, respect, and protection and promise to help them in any way we can.

SUGGESTIONS FOR CHANGE. Write down a list of your hopes and dreams for your children and for yourself as a parent. Include the reasons that you want to be a parent at all. Then make a pledge to your children. Share these lists with them to let them know how important they are in your life.

Once you have your lists, refine them into a plan you actually carry out. Keep in mind that a plan that will hold up under the stresses of real family life needs satisfactory solutions to two problems:

- How to convey to your children the legacy you want for them
- How to nourish your own soul

Choose Loving Solutions

Love is our assignment—the very nature of who we are as human beings commands us to love God and to love our neighbors as ourselves. This is the great Judeo-Christian commandment. The Golden Rule builds on this same understanding of what sustains human community and is at the heart of the teachings of many of the world's great religions.[16] In secular terms we are called to love life and treasure each other and ourselves. This call bears directly on raising healthy children. When love is the foundation for action, the outcome is loving and respectful relationships. Loving families spill love and joy into the friendships and communities surrounding them. Love generates spiritual renewal, just as surely as family feuds generate despair and violence. The problem we face is how to make respect and love the foundation for our family's patterns of relating to each other.

After months of struggle the McGraths had a breakthrough:

Kenny: I had a good time with the kids last weekend. Did they tell you about it?

Jeanne: Sarah said the three of you sewed big sheets together. I didn't know you could sew.

Kenny: *(smiling)* Neither did I. Sarah got pretty good at it.

Jeanne: Then you took them to a park?

Kenny: Yeah, we laid it out on the ground near where some other kids were playing. Sarah got them to hold the edge of the sheet and they started shaking it all together. They got it to billow up like a real parachute. Then they got under it and fell down and it covered them. They were all giggling and laughing. They got up and did it again and again for two hours. Sarah got Rusty doing it and I even tried it a few times. We had a good time.

Jeanne: You amaze me! I'd like to go with you next time you go parachuting.

A short time later Jeanne invited Kenny to talk about getting back together again.

Every Conflict Is a Chance to Teach Better Skills

Conflicts present us with important opportunities. Think about each trouble situation as a chance to model what you want your children to do. Find ways to define and resolve conflict so that all parties grow stronger and more respectful of each other. When you define a family problem so that the basic needs of each person are respectfully included, your clarity serves everyone. Invite your children into this process early on and their enthusiasm for the solutions you choose together will grow.

Be aware that our best intentions can be defeated by our own misbehavior. It's always wise to model the behavior you want in return. Ask yourself how a situation can reinforce your children's self-esteem and compassion for others.

SUGGESTIONS FOR CHANGE. Identify a conflict you would like to change, then answer these questions about it:

- Whose needs are being met by continuing this conflict?
- What needs are being met?
- Who loses out each time? And what needs go unmet?
- How might everyone's needs be met? Think creatively. Make sure this solution builds self-esteem for your children *and* you.

Defining Problems to Create Solutions

For the Durrens, the problems that arose from Jeremy's shoplifting were different for each member of his family.

Jeremy saw the problem as making a poor choice on an impulse that was not meant to hurt anyone. He could have framed it differently. Had he chosen to define the problem as the store treating him unfairly or as him being the victim of his friends' wayward influences, the scenario would have changed dramatically for him and for his family.

It would have also changed if Jeremy's parents had defined it as their moral failure instead of as a brief adolescent excursion out of bounds.

Framing the problem as an adolescent lapse in judgment helped Paula to quiet her ghost feelings of helplessness and shame. Germaine intuitively defined his problem as an unwanted replay of his own struggles with his authoritarian father.

Automatic responses from our childhood frame current problems with outdated information and ideas. If we find ourselves repeating mistakes, we need to reframe the problems so we act differently to solve them.

Respectful, loving, and encouraging attitudes will always work better than critical, shaming, and angry ones when the desired outcome is loving and respectful relationships with each other. Habitual patterns of critical, angry, and avoidant responses to conflict fuel family feuds like kerosene on a fire. The way we treat each other on the journey to healing has to model the healthy family interactions we want or we will subvert our own efforts.

STEP 4

CREATE THE FAMILY CULTURE YOU WANT

Old habits die hard. To end bad habits,

families need compelling new ways to get along.

Mutual respect, good humor, and generous

listening must replace intimidation,

humiliation, and getting even.

IN STEP 1 you were invited to lead a healing process for your family. In Step 2 you started locating the roots of your family's pain. In Step 3 you sharpened your skills and began strengthening yourself to succeed as a healer in your family. Now, in Step 4, you will put all this preparation to work to create a family atmosphere of happiness, love, and understanding for all of you.

Chapters 10 through 18 present building blocks for *creating healthy change.* They are based on my thirty years of work with troubled children, abused and abusive adults, and troubled families, as well as the pleasures and misadventures my wife and I had in raising our two sons.

Part IV begins with "Gentleness and Tenacity" (chapter 10) and "Encouraging Humor" (chapter 11), the backbone of good parenting. If you can develop a patient, good-natured, supportive approach to your personal and family problems, then you'll have a chance to stay in the struggle long enough to win. Understanding that longstanding family problems have deep roots and will not yield easily will help you to avoid underestimating just how hard and how long you will need to work to gain the harmony you want. Chapters 12 through 18 can be read in any order that suits you. These chapters describe the overlapping and interactive parts of an overall strategy for parenting active, happy, and loving children. We need to integrate these approaches into our own personal styles of parenting if we are to fully realize their power to heal old wounds and (in the words of the Convention on the Rights of the Child) create "the family atmosphere of happiness, love, and understanding" we are striving for.

Chapter 10

GENTLENESS AND TENACITY

Exhaustion stalks parents all the time. Choosing your burdens carefully and gently pacing yourself will help you accomplish goals that were out of reach before.

If you downplay or deny the strain of your daily responsibilities and the anxieties that go with them, then you may well exhaust yourself, perhaps before you realize it. Especially with more than one child at home under school age, a chronically ill child, or a seemingly incorrigible one, the strain can quickly build up. Add in a spouse you're having tensions with or who doesn't fully participate in parenting and you may feel ready for a rest home. And these problems will be even worse if you are burdened by your own legacies of absent or abusive parents.

To survive as a good parent, you need to take time to care well for yourself. We all possess an innate resilience. Include on your daily to-do list activities that nourish your soul and recharge your emotional reserves.

Sally always loved to read. Throughout her childhood she would retreat to her room with a book to get away from the hubbub and frequent fighting in her family. Now as a parent with three small children she found it nearly impossible to be alone. When her husband got home from work he wanted her attention, too. One evening she realized that her reward for trying so hard to do everything her family asked her to do was a deep fatigue and rising frustration. The next evening she gave her husband a big hug and a kiss when he got home, told him dinner was on the stove and the kids were watching television, and said she was going to take a hot bath, wash her hair, and curl up in bed with a book she'd been wanting to read for weeks. Three hours later when her husband came to bed, Sally was feeling calmer, refreshed, and sleepy. In the morning she told him they had to find a way she could be alone for at least an hour every day. He agreed to take care of the children for an hour in the evening, which he realized meant saving some energy he'd normally spend at work.

Practicing Gentleness

A parent's life is always overloaded with demands. The only way to create space for your own needs is to conserve your energy. Treat your energy like a precious commodity. Don't waste it where you get no return. Beating yourself up is one example of wasted energy. Some people say horrible things to themselves, like "You stupid idiot" or "I'm such a failure" or "I can't do anything right." Every time you allow yourself such negative self-talk, you waste precious energy. Identify specifically what you're upset about and choose something better to do next time a similar situation occurs. Instead of berating yourself, use the same energy to figure out better choices and ways to exercise those choices. The gentler you can be with yourself about your mistakes, the more likely you'll have enough energy to try new ideas. If your new ideas don't work, you can review what you tried with a friend or a professional and come up with something different to try.

Being gentle with yourself means maintaining an open, relaxed, and nurturing attitude toward your own needs and those of your family. Doing so will put you in a better mood with more energy to face your daily demands. If you can, treat yourself to a daily fifteen-minute meditation where you relax in an atmosphere of gentleness, beauty, and slower time. If you feel too frazzled to carve out a time like this during the day, try using your bedtime or waking-up time.

Imagine yourself in a favorite place where you are warm, relaxed, and free of demands. Pamper yourself in your imagination with whatever feels refreshing. Feel yourself breathe in new energy as you let the tensions flow out of your body and mind. Reserve this time for renewing yourself—problems can wait. This is your way of staying ahead of the demands in your life.

When you are ready to return to the buzz of your life, allow yourself enough time to put your armor back on.

Gentleness means taking it easy sometimes. Back away from your problems and savor the beauty around you. Give yourself permission to relax and recover a little. Be open to the truth about your behavior and work on fixing it with patience and tolerance. The cruelest among us still has the capacity to grow up—to admit to our own rage and to heal through honesty, determination, and the gentleness inspired by remembering how precious newborn children, including us, always are.

Gentleness carries a message of love to our children and to us: Gather what you need for yourself without violating others. Take time-outs. Take nourishment. Take charge. And do what you know will make your family a safe haven for everyone.

Gentleness communicates reverence for the people we love and respect and conveys our intent to keep good judgment, love, and clear thinking ahead of jealousy and anger.

Gentleness acts like a social lubricant to reduce emotional friction so we don't burn out.

Gentleness helps us tolerate others' ideas and ways of doing things, rather than demanding to be in charge all the time.

Gentleness helps us know when to let go or lighten up and calls us to carry our determination quietly.

Gentleness lightens our hearts and inspires those around us to greater kindness. It is a discipline that focuses our emotional attention on what is good and true and enduring in our lives.

Gentleness is a call to reconnect with those we love most and to put aside our squabbles in favor of affirming what is best between us.

Gentleness is one of the faces of generosity. It acts like a shock absorber for family tension. You will travel the road of parenthood more happily and resolve your conflicts more completely when your relationships are nurtured with a robustly gentle regard for one another.

Maintaining an open, relaxed, and loving attitude is a mainstay in my professional toolbox. A gentle frame of mind helps me to respect the complexity of another person's problems and gives me the patience to let her or him decide what happens next.

> **SUGGESTIONS FOR CHANGE.** Find a quiet, comfortable place and close your eyes. Imagine that someone who loves you is cradling you in his or her arms, singing softly, and gently rocking you. Allow yourself to relax and soak up the feeling for ten minutes or as long as you can maintain the image. Remember the feeling so you can call it up to nurture yourself at other times.

Developing Tenacity

The problems we are trying to solve have been sources of family pain perhaps for generations. Shortcuts, temper tantrums, or withdrawal aren't likely to help. Instead, loving perseverance provides the staying power we need to resolve seemingly intractable family tensions.

Understanding our dilemmas is only a half measure to displace old habits. Effective actions to create the new realities we want must follow consistently. This requires tenacity. People come to me saying they know what to do and they know their strategies will work if only they could carry them out. They hire me to teach them how to persevere with their own wisdom. Strategies for developing tenacity share a common thread—they acknowledge that habits are hard to break. We are in a marathon, not a sprint.

Tenacity in pursuing a goal is a key indicator of mental health. It usually develops from years of encouragement and practice. Losing the ability to sustain purposeful activity is an early sign of a mental disorder and a red flag calling us to seek professional help. Raising healthy children is one activity certain to test your ability to persevere.

We have to outlast the hold of old mental and behavioral habits. The corrosive experiences from our earlier lives will continue to intrude on us unless we can stare them down and choose a new response. This is emotional ghost busting. We must face our ghosts no matter how scary they are and send them to an appropriate resting place. With clear goals instead of ghosts and a workable strategy for tenaciously pursuing your goals, you will succeed.

Jeanne's tenacious refusal to put up with Kenny's drunkenness or to give up on their marriage set the stage for the reconciliation that followed. Lesser determination would have resulted in divorce or endless quarreling.

Tenacity is a healthy stubbornness about getting what you need to be healthy and whole.

Helen loved gardening. Through a divorce and years of raising difficult children she tenaciously spent time in her garden. It was her therapy time. "Flowers are patient and beautiful," she told me. "They don't talk back. They don't stay out all night. And they don't follow me into the bathroom." Gardening nurtured her sense of well-being and self-control, and her garden became a sanctuary for her. She said in jest that it kept her from planting a few of her children underground.

Jeff needed a change of pace from the stresses of building a successful business and living with a severely mentally retarded daughter. He loved cycling, a passion he shared with his son. They decided to ride across the United States on a fund-raising mission for the American Diabetes Association. Getting ready gave them many opportunities to work and talk together. Cycling across country became a highlight of Jeff's life. He returned feeling strong, confident, and relaxed. Family tensions seemed easier to handle, and his part in them changed as he was able to meet many of the demands that before had left him exasperated.

Learning what will restore your loving, patient, good-humored disposition, then tenaciously pursuing what you learn—that's what healing yourself is all about.

SUGGESTIONS FOR CHANGE. Other people's help is sometimes essential to our ability to persevere. Identify two people you can enlist to support you in implementing the changes you choose to make. They might be family members or carefully chosen friends. Outline what you want them to do. With clear instructions and appropriate thank-yous, even a four-year-old can hold you to your resolutions. In fact, a child will relish the role.

Annette knew her work in the law office was taking its toll on her nerves. The difficulties faced by her clients, peer pressures, performance anxieties in court, and the volumes of information she had to absorb all would have been hard enough. But she was also a single mother. Her saving grace was Lilly, her four-year-old daughter. Lilly was incorrigibly cheerful. Annette had taught her not to take personally her mother's mistakes. So when Annette came home exhausted and snapped at Lilly, Lilly just frowned and shot back, "Did you have a bad day, Mommy?" She would bring her mom her slippers and talk about her day at her dad's or her grandmother's, and before long Annette was smiling in spite of her day. All this followed the care Annette took in explaining to Lilly that her mom had a very hard job that made her cranky sometimes and Lilly should never take that personally. If Lilly wasn't sure whether she had done something to arouse her mother's anger, she was taught to question her mother further. If Annette was really upset with Lilly, then Annette had to say so clearly in terms Lilly could understand. Lilly felt good when she helped her mother feel better. Yet there was no question about who was really the mother. Annette had the final say.

In the end you will succeed if you don't let your disabling doubts get the best of you. Construct a web of tough and loving relationships to act as a golden cage around your weaknesses. In time you will discover a blend of internal determination and external support that will keep your healing process alive.

Chapter 11

ENCOURAGING HUMOR

I don't know any successful parent who completely lacks a sense of humor. A parent's job is too complex and demanding to survive without the ability to laugh at ourselves when parenting inevitably gets the better of us. We don't need to be professional comedians to see ways we make our own lives harder sometimes. We will feel better and rebound more quickly if we can laugh with our family and say, "Yeah, that was pretty goofy."

Dick Gregory is a professional comedian who routinely has his audiences in stitches of laughter. He mastered the art of using humor to spotlight and heal social and racial tensions. He writes in his autobiography that he learned to be funny as a way to avoid beatings from older and bigger kids.

> I got picked on a lot around the neighborhood; skinniest kid on the block, the poorest, the one without a Daddy. I guess that's when I first began to learn about humor, the power of a joke.[17]

He discovered that if he pre-empted verbal assaults from the bullies, he could capture their interest and then their respect. As a result, he got to be the king of his neighborhood. Pretty soon kids from other neighborhoods came to challenge his ability to make a joke.

Obviously, Gregory has a special talent. But parents don't have to be professional comedians to use humor. Gentle irony and quirky perspectives help us to soothe injured feelings, to create a gentler atmosphere, to take ourselves a little less seriously at times, and to see new ways to solve our conflicts.

A simple strategy to defuse tension is to take up the other side of an argument. Just start arguing for the same side your "opponent" is arguing and see how long it takes him or her to figure it out.

During an argument, enjoy what is going on. Appreciate the skill and energy people are using to oppose each other. Place bets on who is going to win an argument. Narrate an argument you are witnessing as if you were a horse race announcer. If you do it with good humor without belittling anyone, you can reshape the emotional environment and make fighting seem out of place. It is difficult to stay angry with respectful people who stay good-natured. If the situation feels dangerous, then definitely be discreet.

Gregory, who is black, talks about what it takes to be funny when his audience is mostly white and potentially hostile.

> I've got to hit them fast, before they can think, just the way I hit those kids back in St. Louis who picked on me because I was raggedy and had no Daddy. I've got to go up there as an individual first, a Negro second. I've got to be a colored funny man, not a funny colored man. I've got to act like a star who isn't sorry for himself—that way, they can't feel sorry for me. I've got to make jokes about myself, before I can make jokes about them and their society—that way, they can't hate me. Comedy is friendly relations.[18]

Like Gregory, to use humor effectively we parents need to joke about ourselves first to make sure our audience is with us. That way when we joke with our children they don't feel singled out. The humor is evenhanded and has a chance to be accepted when it's needed to defuse family tensions. Good humor is affirming and relieves tension. If it gets ugly, then it's just another stick for beating someone up.

In a family, humor is a state of mind more than funny lines. It's looking for the unexpected angle on situations, being mischievous, and refusing to be serious about whose turn is it to do the dishes. It's boldly changing subjects when old fights break out, and it's telling stories that draw the focus away from bickering and onto something interesting to the people present.

Good humor is about mutual respect and affection. Dick Gregory will tell you it takes a lot of practice, especially when the audience is hostile. In your family spend time to helping each other lighten up, teaching your children to view events with humility. Show them—by not taking yourself too seriously—that they don't have to get worked up over little things. When you need to get serious, they will know by contrast that something is important and they need to pay attention.

A significant shift in family tensions took place when the McGraths started using humor to break old patterns of anger and frustration. I overheard Jeanne tell Kenny in my waiting room that she had a special meeting she needed to attend the next morning. She asked Kenny if he could take Sarah to school. He put on a burdened look and said, "I don't think there's any way I could . . ." and then he smiled and ended with "refuse to do that." Jeanne realized she was being teased, and she smiled. When I realized that Kenny had said yes with no strings attached, I added my own silent but emphatic "Yes!"

SUGGESTIONS FOR CHANGE. Pick one recurrent conflict situation, say, getting your child to do the dishes. Now imagine that you are up on a balcony looking down on yourself and your child fighting as usual. Keep this picture in your mind and start to laugh at yourself for getting sucked in by a child. As you recognize the comedy in the situation, you'll begin to smile—you may even laugh out loud. Now that you're in a better mood and not in the middle of an argument, you can probably think of a different approach to getting the chore completed. Try it next time and see what happens.

Chapter 12

RECRUITING ALLIES

Once we accept our role in recreating our childhood family pain—that is, once we can see it and say with humility "There I go again"—we can take the next step toward healing that pain by inviting our family partners to join us on the journey of healing. Just don't expect too much of them too soon. They may be more resistant to change than we were. In fact, we are very likely to hear complaints like

- What right do you have to demand that we change?
- How dare you abandon our usual ways of doing things!
- You're making everyone anxious and upset!

Don't allow this expected backlash to deter you. Remember that *families are closed systems*—anything that happens to anyone in a family affects everyone else in the family. When you acknowledge your own fears and mistakes to benefit the family, you create an atmosphere of opportunity for some and vulnerability for others. Meaningful change challenges the family status quo, and anyone benefiting from the way the family operated before is likely to object. Change puts the spotlight on power struggles in the family. Your task will be to nudge everyone toward win-win resolutions of old wars.

Win-Win Strategies

Create the expectation that every family member will be treated with love and respect. Someone left out or injured by a so-called solution will work to undermine it, and scapegoats will provoke new conflicts to get even or to win something next time. We call these *win-lose solutions* because while somebody got what he or she wanted, someone else was left feeling cheated. Resentments then build into a new confrontation that will invite another win-lose "solution," and on goes the chronic family fighting.

Mrs. Andrews grew up the younger of two sisters, suffering for years in her sister's shadow. Nothing successfully relieved her feelings of inferiority and resentment. At the birth of her own second daughter, she promised herself that this daughter would not suffer on account of her older sister. Consequently, as her girls grew up Mrs. Andrews stepped between her younger daughter, Beth, and older daughter, Margie, in ways that left Margie feeling unfairly treated: "Beth is Mom's favorite. It doesn't matter who started it, it's always my fault." Every time the dishes or the laundry needed washing, there was a fight about who did it last. Margie usually was held responsible and her resentments grew. "It's not fair," she said. "You're older," her mother replied, "and I expect you to be more responsible." At school Margie started telling Beth's friends that Beth was the child of an affair their mother had. If she couldn't get her mother's ear, she would get even through Beth's friends.

A family member who repeatedly comes away from family conflicts feeling cheated, humiliated, or injured will invariably create new conflicts for the rest of the family. That is why *win-win* strategies are necessary if conflict is to stop.

Mrs. Andrews spoke with a friend about her frustrations with Beth and Margie. The friend recognized that Mrs. Andrews was siding with Beth at Margie's expense and suggested she try being more even-handed. So Mrs. Andrews tried reasoning with the two of them: "Can't you two work out a way to get the dishes washed every night?" But that just started another argument. Next she tried guilt: "If you two don't stop fighting, you're going to drive me into the hospital." Her friend then suggested that Mrs. Andrews come to see me.

Mrs. Andrews:	I can't stand this.
Dr. Hall:	I understand you and your older sister were rivals, too.
Mrs. Andrews:	We still don't talk to each other.
Dr. Hall:	Why is that?
Mrs. Andrews:	I used to hate her. Now I just don't think about her. I always thought she hated me from the way she made fun of me in front of our friends. She spread the meanest rumors about me. And when I told Mom about it, my sister called me all kinds of names. If Mom hadn't stopped her, I think she would have killed me.
Dr. Hall:	Relate this to the situation with your daughters now.
Mrs. Andrews:	*(laughs)* Margie is ready to kill Beth, and maybe I'm the one to blame. I can feel how quickly I come to Beth's rescue, even when I'm not sure who started the trouble. But the urge to protect Beth is so strong, I'm not sure I can not do it.
Dr. Hall:	Perhaps it's time to give Beth the chance to stand up for herself and let the two of them work out their differences without you.
Mrs. Andrews:	But what if Margie really gets angry and takes it out on Beth?
Dr. Hall:	If you're worried that Beth can't stand up for herself, then you'd better teach her what to do. I doubt it's in her best interest to always need her mother.

Some time later Mrs. Andrews told me her daughters were getting along better, although they still had many loud arguments. A truce was holding between them. Margie had a fair chance to protect herself from her sister's attacks, Beth had a chance to build her self-confidence, and Mrs. Andrews had a new degree of freedom.

Finding Allies

Win-win solutions can be hard to find in families that have been at odds for a long time. In such families, unspoken rules protect some members of the family from fair consequences for their misbehaviors while others take the blame for problems they have no power to control. If family members are to break out of a pattern like this, they will need a clear, strong advocate for a new model of fair consequences. And they will need allies within the family. Otherwise, their only hope will be to escape the family altogether. The letter below is offered as an example of the language one may need to use with other members of the family in order to break free of the unjust patterns that have created trouble for so long.

Often one's spouse or adult partner is the most difficult person to bring along on a campaign for change. And the children who align themselves with that partner will likewise resist. Your job is to convince them it is in their best interest also to make the changes you advocate. The threat that you will leave is obviously a measure of last resort, but knowing that you can and will leave may be a crucial element of your power to create change. Your partner will realize you are serious about changing the old ways of not getting along. (If you recurrently threaten to leave and never do, you face the dilemma of the boy who cried wolf—no one will take you seriously. So use this tactic only as a last resort.) If real love holds your family together, you will get the attention you seek. If not, you may realize you don't really want to stay anyway. This is something for you to figure out *before* you create the havoc that demanding change can bring. If the following letter truly speaks for you, then you are ready to battle for a new order in your family. If you're not sure, give yourself time to develop the clarity and strength you will need before pressing your case.

A Sample Letter to My Partner:

We have allowed ourselves to mistreat each other for long enough. I want us to make our relationship fundamentally better or I want a separation. I can no longer tolerate the old assaults on each other that have been our habit. Let us love and respect each other. If we cannot, then let us separate as friends.

In hope,
Your Partner

With a statement like this you begin a nonviolent campaign against the old order of win-lose fighting. Expect opposition. An upstaged partner will be very resourceful and may use some or all of his or her timeworn strategies for bringing you back into line with the old family order. This resistance is normal and nearly inevitable. So be ready to stand against it strongly enough and long enough to succeed with the changes you want to bring about.

Play fair according to mutually beneficial rules. Don't waste energy with idle threats you have no intention of carrying out. And keep inviting other family members into the loving pursuit of healing.

Occasionally, extended family members and even close friends become embroiled in the struggle to save the old order. If this happens, decide as a family if they truly belong in your family's inner circle. If they do, treat them as a member of the family and hold them accountable for their roles in the old order and the new. If they do not belong, tell them clearly and firmly to respect your need for family privacy.

Treat your partners (adult and child) as if they are already allies in your plans for healing. Listen when they raise objections. Acknowledge the truth in what they say. Help solve the problems they raise. Make the process work for them and for you. If they still don't join in, then continue to educate them about how your life together will improve with win-win ways of relating. The strength of your position rests with the strength of the options you can choose. Your job in leading the healing process is to identify win-win ways to travel with your partners in a direction you all want to go.

Wendy and Brian came to see me shortly after he slapped her for the first time in their eighteen-year marriage. They argued and yelled frequently over the years, often about their now seventeen-year-old daughter, Stephanie, and fifteen-year-old son, Michael. This argument escalated after Stephanie missed her 10 P.M. curfew. When Stephanie hadn't called by 10:30 P.M., Wendy started to panic.

> Brian: Wendy, don't worry so much. Stephanie's old enough to fend for herself.
>
> Wendy: But what if she's in a car wreck somewhere? What if she's gotten herself messed up with those boys again?
>
> Brian: Just leave it alone. She'll get here when she gets here. We will talk with her then.

(Wendy's anxiety kept mounting. She began pacing between the kitchen and living room.)

> Brian: *(irritated)* Would you please stop pacing and go to bed?
>
> Wendy: I can't help it. I'm worried about her.
>
> Brian: We've been through this many times before and she always comes home.
>
> Wendy: Yes, but what if this time—
>
> Brian: *(interrupting)* Stop it!
>
> Wendy: *(bursting into tears and yelling in Brian's face)* Don't speak to me like that.

Wendy slammed the bedroom door and locked herself in. Brian paced the living room for an hour before falling asleep. When Stephanie came in at 2 A.M., Wendy screamed at her, "Where have you been?" Stephanie recoiled, burst into tears, and slammed her own bedroom door.

Reconciliation in this family took many months. When they first came to see me, both Brian and Wendy felt abused and ready to quit. My task was to help them see each other again as allies and their hurt feelings as a common problem to solve together. Several early sessions were devoted to giving each one a forum to share his or her individual pain. As each felt better understood, the tensions relaxed. They both reaffirmed their longstanding love for each other, apologized for letting the situation explode, and agreed to counseling for anxiety and anger.

Once they were again working together they brought Stephanie and Michael into therapy. Stephanie had withdrawn from the family since the explosion and Michael had become irritable and obnoxious at home.

> *Brian:* Stephanie, we've told you we were sorry for the way things went that night. So why won't you talk with us?

(Stephanie doesn't answer.)

> *Michael:* She's still pissed off that Mom screamed at her like that.

> *Wendy:* I'm truly sorry I yelled at you like that. What more do you want?

> *Stephanie:* Yelled? You *screamed* at me!

> *Brian:* What's wrong?

> *Stephanie:* I just need to get away from you guys. I wish I was graduated already, then I could leave and not have to deal with the way you baby me all the time.

> *Wendy:* I get worried about you. I know what can happen at your age.

> *Stephanie:* You're such a worrywart. I can take care of myself. If I want to stay out at night, I can. And you can't stop me.

Brian:	If you won't come home on time, we'll have to take away the car.
Stephanie:	So? I'll get my friends to drive me.
Dr. Hall:	I suspect there's a lot of tension like this at home.
Stephanie:	It's unbearable.
Dr. Hall:	I assume that no one likes it this way. What might any of you do to stop it?
Wendy:	It would help if Stephanie wasn't so rebellious.
Dr. Hall:	What is your part in creating this tension?
Wendy:	I get so anxious I feel I'm having a nervous break-down sometimes.
Dr. Hall:	What can you do to reduce your anxiety?
Wendy:	I've tried meditation and a relaxation tape, and they helped for a little while.
Dr. Hall:	Perhaps your anxiety is more severe than that. Would you be open to an evaluation for a possible trial of medicine?
Wendy:	If you think it would help.

We worked together to identify the family's problems and to frame them as problems in common that needed everyone's help. When Stephanie would get huffy about putting up with her mother's high anxiety, someone would remind her that she was making it worse and that she would benefit from helping her mother to reduce the anxiety. When Michael started wanting to stay out late with his friends, someone would remind him to plan it out ahead of time so his parents could be comfortable and give him the freedom he wanted.

You May Need to Walk Away

Sometimes a powerful but inattentive member of your family requires a wake-up call. If your family atmosphere has soured and your family member remains unresponsive, you might need to increase the pressure.

An early step in creating family change is the assessment of your power to create that change. Knowing what you can do sometimes prevents others from pushing you that far.

The ultimate power you can wield is to leave and possibly take the children with you. This has to be an option or you allow yourself to stay in a potentially deadly win-lose trap. If you are not prepared to leave when your partner (usually a spouse but other family members too) flatly refuses to cooperate, then you lose the leverage to make the partnership work. If you must stay in your relationship no matter what, then your partner is free to treat you any way he or she likes. You need to know under what circumstances you would separate. Honesty is essential. If you fool yourself about what you will do, you invite failure. Your partner will call your bluff. Choose your actions thoughtfully so you can follow through on the consequences you promise. This means carrying out a tough and assertive plan within the rules of love and respect. This may be what it takes to dislodge entrenched ghosts from within your relationship. This is sometimes what it takes to create win-win outcomes out of win-lose legacies.

Jeanne exercised her option to separate from Kenny and stayed away for two years. That's what it took to get his attention. There was no hope he would get the message if she stayed.

It is said that if you want the cooperation of a Missouri mule, you have to get his attention first by hitting him over the head. This is not a license to hit somebody but rather notice that you must sometimes be emphatic in order to be taken seriously.

Once your partner knows you will leave if he or she forces you to leave, then your less drastic options acquire new strength. Now that you have your partner's attention you can negotiate in earnest: "I would rather stay and work things out, but I need your help. I can't do it alone. Do I have your attention now? Or do you really want me to leave?"

Halfway Home

If there's enough love and respect left so your threat to leave gets your partner's attention rather than his or her vote for a separation, you have a chance to develop the partnership you will need for addressing recurrent family problems. Once you succeed in gaining an active partner in the healing process, the battle for a healthy family is half won. Two working together will in time overcome the obstacles that legacies, a mental disorder, temperament, or culture throw in your way.

Practice the Rules

Start by agreeing to follow the rules for fair fighting (see page 120). Following these rules won't come naturally—you are establishing new patterns and new habits. You may not get much cooperation, and initial efforts often prove disappointing. Time and practice will make everyone more aware and comfortable with these rules and the benefits they provide. When in doubt, walk in each other's shoes for a while. I will occasionally invite people in my office to swap chairs and role-play each other. That way they are forced to some degree to imagine what it's like to be the other person. Usually this helps people find more understanding and common ground.

The first time Jeanne and Kenny tried these rules on their own they lasted about three minutes before Jeanne gave up. She said Kenny was not listening when it was her turn to talk. When they tried it in my office, it became clear that Kenny thought paraphrasing what Jeanne had said just meant saying similar words back to her. So the next exercise for them was to paraphrase what each had heard *using the same emphasis and meaning with which the other said it.* There's an important difference between saying the same words and conveying the same meaning. For example, Jeanne had told Kenny, "I'm too tired to put up with your drinking anymore." What Kenny initially paraphrased back to her was, "You don't want me around anymore." She had to correct him, "No, I do want you around but only if you can get your drinking under control." Even as they improved their communication, the tendency to begin arguing was difficult to restrain. These dynamics changed when Kenny discovered that talking matters through could work in his favor, too, and he began to listen *in order to understand* what he heard.

SUGGESTIONS FOR CHANGE. Choose a situation that repeatedly creates tension or arguments and bring the principal players together (see Ground Rules for a Family Discussion on page 37 for help in setting this up) for a test run of the rules for fair fighting. Try them out. Afterward, ask everyone what worked and what didn't work. Try again right away or agree to reconvene later.

Dealing with a Controlling Partner

One reason rules for fair fighting don't work in some families is that one partner is committed to controlling every family interaction. This can present you with a special and potentially dangerous predicament. The usual rules for fair fighting are not acceptable to someone who always needs to win. If this is true in your family, the following suggestions for identifying and dealing with someone who is overcontrolling may help you.

SUGGESTIONS FOR CHANGE. Answer these questions to see more clearly how much your partner tries to control you.

- How readily does your partner stop when you say "Stop"?
- How freely can you choose your friends and when and where to meet them?
- Are you free to pursue your own career interests?
- Does your partner share fully in childcare and household chores?
- Does your partner intimidate you?

Excessive control and abuse begin where consent ends. The hallmark of abuse is the abuser's relentless demand for control. If this feels like your family, see appendix E for more help.

RULES FOR FAIR FIGHTING

George Bach and Peter Wyden in *The Intimate Enemy* were the first to introduce me to rules for fair fighting.[19] Here is my edited summary.

The parties to a conflict agree to the following:

1. A time and place to fight (within 48 hours)
2. No one assaults people or property
3. An appropriate time limit (5 to 90 minutes)
4. Equal time for each party
    * Speak to inform
    * Listen to understand
5. A time and place for the next round (within 48 hours)

Apply the rules uniformly. Adults and children are equally bound by the rules. Parents have the final say, of course, but must model with their own behavior what they want from others. This is a time to practice the Golden Rule. Treat others as you want them to treat you. Encourage people to air painful feelings in ways that increase understanding and ease the pain without attacking anyone.
Stick to the rules. Intervene to stop a physical assault and also to stop cruel comments to someone unprepared to deal with them. Otherwise, let the people talk.

Chapter 13

TREASURING YOUR CHILDREN

Our children are among creation's exquisite achievements. As exasperating as they can be at times, treasuring them is our joy and our job. Tenacious love brings out their cooperation in ways anger and criticism cannot. Quiet awe at the mystery of their existence nudges us toward self-restraint and good humor. They are exquisite, like the lilies of the field. Awareness of their splendor helps buffer any frustration we feel with them.

Kenny's daughter, Sarah, was at the center of his emotional pain throughout his separation.

Kenny: Doc, there are nights I sit in my empty apartment and ask myself, How did I get kicked out like this? I have this nightmare sometimes that Sarah is going away from me in a car. She's crying and there's nothing I can do to comfort her or stop her from leaving me.

He went over and over the way he would yell at Sarah when he was tired and she was fussy. He remembered how exasperated he felt when he wanted to read to her and she couldn't decide on a story. She would burst into tears and cry to her mother, "Daddy's yelling at me again!" Eventually, Kenny came to believe that his every-other-weekend time with Sarah was too precious to waste on scolding her.

Despite the inevitable hassles, hard work, and heartaches, children also bring a special joy to our lives. We too easily forget how precious and fragile they are. Parental rejection causes them great pain. When we are truly in touch with loving our children, *everything* they do reminds us of what precious gifts they are—smiles or tantrums, anger or cooperation, awards or arrests. Think to yourself, or even say to them out loud, "There are times I don't like what I see you doing. But I always love you. And I love having you in my life." The harder they are to love, the more intentional we may need to be in celebrating them in our lives every day.

Kenny told me he missed his daughter's fussiness almost as much as her smiles.

Kenny: It sounds crazy, but I smile now when she gets fussy, so long as she doesn't do it all the time. I hate being a stranger to my own daughter. The things she did that bugged me don't matter now.

Kenny could have quit being a parent when he was kicked out of the house. He could have become bitter and punished Jeanne and the children. He did for a while. But his better self hated being a drunk and wanted to be a good father.

Failure to Treasure Our Children Causes Great Harm

Treasuring our children is not just a good idea, it has been proven vitally important to their healthy growth and development—and sometimes their very survival. In one of the most striking studies ever done with children, R.A. Spitz studied orphaned infants in London during World War II.[20] Nuns raised them in a sterile environment free of germs, color, and human relationships. The cribs were lined up end to end in a big white room, and the nuns faithfully cared for the infants' physical needs. But none of the infants had an individual attachment to any caregiver. By six months of age an astounding 50 percent of these infants died. Spitz speculated that they died of "nurture failure." Apparently infants need consistent love as much as food if they are to survive. "Failure to thrive" is a pediatric syndrome characterized by seriously slowed physical growth in young children who lack reliable emotional bonding with a primary caregiver.

Older children also need consistent love to fulfill their physical and emotional growth potential. Neglected children show lasting effects of early emotional starvation through their inability to form deep and lasting relationships later on. These children grow up in disproportionate numbers to become school dropouts, unemployed, recipients of public assistance, incarcerated criminals, and patients in psychiatric settings.

Thank Goodness for Our Lovable—and Unruly—Children

Stand in awe of the miracle of life you witness in your children. Tell them individually, "I love you. You are beautiful in my eyes!" Fred Rogers of *Mister Rogers' Neighborhood* on the Public Broadcasting System told children daily for a generation, "I like you just the way you are." This ingenious affirmation hits at the core of what children need—repeated personal assurance that they are good and that someone cares about them. Celebrate your children's toddler-scribble drawings and their flawed young acting debut. Celebrate their insistence on doing laundry all by themselves even if they don't yet know how to do it. Celebrate their lovability when their actions annoy you as well as when they please you. Celebrate how hard they struggle with their homework or cutting their first dress pattern. Celebrate when they stand up to you and tell you that you are wrong. Celebrate them just the way they are—and mean it.

And yes, celebrate them when they are unruly. The younger the child, the more likely unruliness represents fatigue, frustration, a play for attention, or a sense of humor. Celebrate it wherever it comes from!

Praise your children: "You played so hard today. I was exhausted just watching you." Offer comfort: "You wore yourself out. Come lie in my lap."

Celebrate their mischief: "You were sure creative to shake up those soda cans and spray them all over the kitchen! Now let's see how creative we can be in cleaning it up."

These are ready-made opportunities to spend extra time with your children. Put yourself in a good mood. Put the mess in perspective. No one was hurt. No real damage was done. Turn the mess into a cleanup project together. Your good humor sets a model you will much appreciate if you dent the car or forget to pick the children up from school. As your children grow smarter and stronger, your confrontations with them will grow more intense and difficult. Your ability to maintain loving appreciation and good humor while they wrestle with your authority will become ever more crucial to maintaining healthy family ties. Teenagers best strengthen their assertive skills and authority with parents who celebrate their efforts and forgive their transgressions.

SUGGESTIONS FOR CHANGE. When children seek your time, give them your best.

- Listen to them with your full attention.
- Feel their enthusiasm.
- Be glad they're there.
- Plan ways to enjoy time together every day.
- Teach them to negotiate for your time so you can be fully present. ("Right now" is not always the best time for a child to get your full attention.)

Unruliness Is an Attempt to Communicate

Sarah had mixed feelings every time she got to her father's apartment. She was glad to see him and mad at him for being away. She was mad that she had to leave her mom, and she felt her mom's anger at her dad. She needed the reassurance of consistency. She wanted the same foods that her mom fixed. When Kenny didn't fix the right food or fix it the right way, she would pout or have a tantrum. Over time Kenny learned to celebrate her moodiness, both because he was so genuinely glad to see her after two weeks and because he now understood that she was legitimately angry with him for leaving her. He also learned enough patience to wait out her unruly behavior until he better understood what she needed him to know.

As our children mature, their ability to drive us crazy should mature as well. Teenagers are notorious for sullenness, passive resistance, back talk, and outright defiance. We can learn to celebrate this, too. They need tenacious love and support in order to weather their developmental storms. Celebrate your children's growing strength and competence.

Jeremy grew up a lot after he was caught shoplifting. Rather than follow through on the first idea he came up with, he thought about how the action might turn out. Money seemed more real to him after paying the $250 fine. He was now keenly aware that his parents could be hurt by his decisions and nonetheless would solidly support him no matter what he did. In appreciation and with a sense of relief he settled back into school, the school band, and the track team.

Self-Esteem Is Built by Age Six

Child development research tells us clearly that the foundations for self-esteem and self-discipline are laid in the first three to six years of life. These are crucial years to give children confidence in their lovability and competence. Children who are loved no matter how frustrating their behavior is will grow up with a good chance for liking themselves and liking other people.

A PARENTS' MANIFESTO

- I may not always agree with what you do, but I dedicate my life to giving you a chance to grow up and make your own choices.
- I will be someone you can depend on.
- I will love you no matter how poorly you respond to my wishes.
- I will work to modify my troublesome behavior and yours.
- I will model love and respect and hope you will love in return.

Joey Hazen was a difficult fifteen-year-old to get to know. He remained sullen and uncommunicative through the few sessions he attended. Margaret spoke openly about how she tried to see Joey as his own person, separate from his father. Joey and eleven-year-old Jonathan both were present with Margaret for this exchange.

Margaret: (to me) Joey can't seem to leave the little ones alone when he's home, and when he's out, I don't know where he is or what he's doing.

Joey: It's none of your business.

Margaret: I'm your mother. It's my business to know where you are.

Joey:	What do you care anyway? Half the time you don't even get my name right.
Margaret:	I call you "Bubba" *(Joey's dad's nickname)*. What's wrong with that?
Joey:	Mom, that's Dad's name, not mine. You gave me my own name. Use it. You don't give a rip about me. You just want my old man back and you can't have him so you pretend he's here anyway.

(Margaret looked at me in despair.)

Dr. Hall:	*(to Margaret)* I know you don't mean to hurt Joey, but the fact is you keep mentioning little things that remind you both of Joey's father. Joey gets frustrated and resentful. Actually he seems pretty restrained and respectful for someone who is regularly slapped with words by his own mother.

(Margaret slumped this time as Joey sat up straighter.)

Joey:	Mom, I'm sorry, but I can't stand to be around you.
Dr. Hall:	Joey, why are you so frustrated with your mom?
Joey:	I wanted to shave my head, but she wouldn't let me.
Dr. Hall:	Why not?
Joey:	I don't know. Ask her.
Dr. Hall:	Why didn't you let Joey shave his head?
Margaret:	He's got all that nice hair. He would look like a criminal without any hair.
Dr. Hall:	Would he look more or less like his father with a shaved head?
Margaret:	His father always had nice hair. I just think Joey would look strange without any hair.
Dr. Hall:	How about letting Joey decide for himself?
Margaret:	That's what you think I should do?
Dr. Hall:	What harm could it do?

Margaret:	What if he gets kicked out of school?
Dr. Hall:	How about it, Joey? Would you get in trouble with a shaved head?
Joey:	They don't care. And so what if they did?
Dr. Hall:	Sounds like something to find out about. How about dying your hair like Dennis Rodman instead? Would that help your mom see you instead of your dad?
Joey:	You gotta be kidding. She'd never let me do that.
Dr. Hall:	How about it, Margaret? Do you prefer Joey shaved bald or red-haired like Dennis Rodman?
Margaret:	Dr. Hall, is that the only choice I have?
Dr. Hall:	How about it, Joey? Are there any other choices she has?
Joey:	*(with a smile)* That's it. Bald or red.
Margaret:	You two are teaming up on me.
Dr. Hall:	Kind of looks like it. Which will it be?
Margaret:	*(beginning to smile)* I think I would rather have him bald. If he goes red and I call him Dennis, I'll be right back in hot water.
Jonathan:	Oh, wow! Joey with a shaved head. All right! Hey, Mom, can I do it, too?
Margaret:	Over my dead body. This one's for Joey only, so don't even think about it.

Our childhood experiments with breaking rules become our testing grounds for personal power, independent thought, and individual responsibility. Our children's attempts to get the better of us become the basis for their assertiveness later on. If we teach them how to challenge us respectfully and successfully, they will gain confidence in their ability to say no to drugs, sex, violence, and injustice in their teenage years and throughout their lives. Their willingness to try new things, even if the immediate result is failure, nourishes their curiosity and creativity for a lifetime of successful problem solving.

You Are So Good at Getting My Goat!

If we support their early efforts at autonomy, our children will reward us by becoming more responsible as they grow older. Obnoxious behavior often has the dual motive of getting our attention and getting our goat.

Sarah threw a fit one night soon after returning home from a weekend visit with her father. Jeanne was getting her ready for bed. Sarah stood by her bed and screamed, "I'm not going to bed, and you can't make me!" She started throwing her clothes on the floor and kicking them around the room.

Jeanne's initial reaction was exasperation, then a surge of fury. In the past she would have snapped back with a comment like "Young lady, you get your pajamas on right now, clean up these clothes, and get into bed or I will paddle you." But Jeanne, too, was grieving the loss of family and knew her short temper helped create the rupture. She took a different approach.

Jeanne: Sarah, honey, I know you are very tired. I am very tired, too. I also know it is really hard on you when you have to go back and forth between Daddy and me.

(Sarah pouted but stopped her tantrum.)

Jeanne: I know you want Daddy to come home so we could all be together again. I am really sorry it is so hard on you. Your daddy loves you. I love you.

(Jeanne moved next to Sarah and tried to put an arm around her.)

(Sarah pulled away and glared.)

Jeanne: It's okay to get mad about our not living together. It's okay to throw your clothes if that's what helps

you to feel better. I will stay and watch if you want me
to, or I will wait for you with a storybook in my room.

Sarah: It's not fair! I hate both of you! *(She threw more clothes
and books.)* Daddy told me it's your fault he can't come
back. He said you're a bad woman.

*(Jeanne lost her temper, grabbed Sarah, and pinned her down on
the bed.)*

Sarah: *(enraged)* You're hurting me! I hate you!

Jeanne held on, wishing for someone to rescue her and Sarah. As
it dawned on her that she was on her own, she remembered to calm
down inside. She maintained a firm grip on Sarah, who continued to
struggle and scream. Eventually Sarah gave in to her mother's
grasp, began to cry, and finally fell asleep.

Sarah was sad and angry. She had lost her intact family and she was
worried she might be the next one her mother ordered to leave. Her
tantrum vented some of her anger, sadness, and hurt. Jeanne managed to control her temper and focus on Sarah's real distress. In that
way she created a win-win bonus for both of them. Even though she
lost her temper for a moment, Jeanne was still able to restrain herself
and Sarah in a way that changed the atmosphere from one of rage to
one of understanding, and Sarah felt her mother's love and strength.

Celebrate Children's Trial-and-Error
Efforts to Be Themselves

Healthy parents want their children to take appropriate responsibility
for themselves as soon as they can do so safely. Children acquire competence as we celebrate their trial-and-error efforts to be themselves.
Help them to try out different ways to relate to other people. Invite
your younger children to pretend to be a mother, a policeman, a movie

star, a waiter, a teacher, a president, or someone else they choose. Let them plan and execute scenarios in play where they are in charge and they choose what you do. At those times when they challenge your authority for real with defiance or noncooperation, watch for signs of the make-believe characters they used to play. The more we affirm their ingenuity and avoid getting hooked by any hostility, the more we can guide our children toward positive emotional growth.

In Sarah's mind her three-and-a-half-year-old brother Rusty was a toy. She carried him around like a big rag doll. Jeanne had to watch them closely because Sarah's mixed feelings toward Rusty stood out like quills on a porcupine. He had four surgeries by age three for cleft palate repair and Sarah felt left out. These operations were highly stressful for the entire family. On one occasion Sarah was curled up on the sofa watching cartoons, hugging Rusty like a teddy bear. She decided she was hungry and stood up so quickly she dropped Rusty on the floor. As she walked to the kitchen, Rusty howled. The phrase "How many times do I have to tell you to be *careful* with your brother?" fumed in Jeanne's mind, but this time she kept quiet. Rusty's bellowing stopped soon enough and clearly he was not injured.

When Jeanne told me about this incident, she explained Sarah's dilemmas this way.

Jeanne: Sarah really loves Rusty, but she was jealous of him from the beginning. It reminded me how jealous I felt of my little sister when we were growing up. When I told Sarah it was okay to feel jealous and I knew she felt lonely and scared when Rusty was in the hospital so long, Sarah told me about sometimes hoping Rusty would die. Then she would be terrified that it might come true. Treating him like he didn't have any feelings or any life of his own was Sarah's way of pretending she didn't have these fears and anger. She cried when she told me and we hugged. After that she became very protective of her little brother. I could relax when the two of them were together and I could finally send them off together to visit their father, which gave me much freer weekends twice a month. Now seeing them together can make my day.

Come Show Me!

When a child is excited about something, we have an ideal chance to celebrate his or her excitement. Encourage your child with your enthusiasm. Time spent now can save you hours of hassles later. Say, "Yes, come show me what you have done! You are wonderful and creative and energetic." Your child will feel proud and important and will want to continue to please you. Children thrive on heartfelt praise. When they have had enough they will let you know. Until then, adore them generously. The child ignored too much develops resentments that fuel tantrums and oppositional behaviors that will take more of your time and energy and deplete your good humor.

Shaming and Blaming Destroy Our Credibility and Our Children

Shaming is a relatively easy way to intimidate children into submission, but it makes our families emotionally toxic. Six-year-old Martin seemed desolate when he came home with his mother one day. She fumed to his father, "Martin did it again! He wet his pants in the grocery store. This time I just announced it to the crowd, 'Look everyone, my six-year-old son just wet his pants.'" Parents need to use the same degree of care and restraint in using shame as they use in hitting their children across the face. Shame is a blunt instrument that destroys our children's self-esteem.

Everyone in Ginny's family was overweight, but in front of her family and friends her father would call her "Wilbur" after the pig in *Charlotte's Web*. Ginny felt humiliated, but even her mother didn't tell her father to stop. Children readily understand that their behavior reflects on their parents. Ginny's father may be surprised when he discovers how much distress Ginny will cause him when she becomes "incorrigible." Perhaps she'll get pregnant at age twelve or thirteen just to humiliate him. She won't care that she humiliates herself, too. She will have retaliated against his callousness and at least chosen her own humiliation this time.

A not-so-subtle variant is to blame our children for the problems we have with them. A classic conflict arises between some pubescent girls and their immature fathers, when the father can't admit his sexual attraction to his daughter and instead berates her for dating and accuses her of being sexually promiscuous. In another common scenario an alcoholic mother accuses her children of driving her to drink: "If you weren't so infuriating, I wouldn't need to get drunk so often." Or a father blames his chronically ill child for the enormous strain of her illness: "If she wasn't sick, I'd be getting enough sleep and I'd still have my job." Strained marriages often crumble when a child is the focus of a family crisis: "If it weren't for how much trouble those kids are, we could work out the problems we have." Blaming children for events beyond their control, like a father's drunkenness or a mother's depression or marital infidelity, consigns the children to helplessness and rage. Blaming them for resisting our assaults is like blaming the horse for bucking after we put a burr under its saddle. Rather than learning from mistakes, children controlled by shaming or blaming come to fear making mistakes and in the process come to fear being themselves. In the worst of these situations we parents blame our children for our own abusiveness: "You just got what was coming to you." When we demean our children in these ways, we can expect them to turn against us with a hostility that will corrode their ability to cooperate with us. (In extreme cases they may even retaliate with suicidal or homicidal rage.)

Devaluing our children shackles them with fears about living their lives. We overload them with poisonous beliefs: "You are worthless." "You are responsible for our family's problems." "There isn't anybody who could love somebody like you." In response to our shaming and blaming they must settle for lives full of rage and depression. The severe emotional disability that goes with these beliefs denies children the possibility of loving relationships just as surely as if we had put them in prison. If we lock them in a real jail, we can at least see the confinement we impose on them. The truth is, many of our incarcerated children carry deep emotional scars.

Anyone who uses shaming and blaming with his or her children has an assignment—stop doing it. Habitual shaming and blaming poisons a family's emotional life and distorts budding personalities.

Shaming and blaming deserve a central place on the trash heap of terrible parenting. Recognizing that we use these approaches does not mean we are bad people. It means we learned some destructive ways to treat each other and we need to learn healthier ways in their place. The antidote to shaming and blaming is to treat every member of the family with love and respect.

Chapter 14

SHARING YOUR STORIES, SHARING YOURSELF

Children weave their family stories into the fabric of their self-esteem. This chapter explores several different ways to share your stories and yourself with your children so they can choose what to make their own and what to leave behind.

Once Upon a Time

Storytelling begins as early as we start talking to our children. Bring alive for your children the spirit of your family as well as the facts. Tell them about where you grew up and where your parents came from. Introduce them to grandparents, aunts and uncles, cousins, and kissing kin. Regale them with the rogues and workers, saints and sinners. Weave your family problems into your stories so your children begin to figure them out. In this way you are giving them a head start on coping with problems that have vexed their relatives.

> When Sarah asked questions about her parents' separation, Jeanne used the occasion to make up a story to help Sarah understand.
>
> Once there were two bears, a momma and a papa bear, and three little bears. They lived together until one day Momma Bear said to Papa Bear, "You have to leave. You've been stealing honey and the bees follow you home and sting us. You'll have to leave until you can leave the beehive alone."

The baby bears were very upset. They loved Papa Bear.

"Why does Papa have to leave?" they asked.

"Because the bees that Papa Bear brings home keep stinging us. That's not good for us. But Papa Bear can't stop doing it."

"We think you're mean," they said.

"Would you like to invite him over?" Momma Bear asked.

"Can we? Can we?" they asked back.

"Okay, but be careful not to let the bees sting you."

So Papa Bear came over. And sure enough, honey dripped from his paws. Bees chased him into the house and went right to stinging the children.

"Ouch! Get them away from me!" they shouted.

"Papa Bear, your children asked to see you, but you brought the bees again. You have to leave right now," Momma Bear said.

"It's not my fault the bees keep following me," Papa Bear said. "I can't tell the bees what to do."

"Get them away!" the children shouted.

So Mama Bear shooed Papa Bear out the door and the bees followed him.

"We don't like the bees," the children said.

"I'm sorry you had to find out the hard way," said Momma Bear.

The children said, "Papa Bear said it wasn't his fault the bees came, but the bees were mad at him for stealing their honey. We won't invite him back again until he stops stealing honey."

The end.

Major family disruptions need plenty of storytelling. What happens to children at two years of age can have a huge impact on their self-esteem even as grownups. If, for example, a parent was absent for many months, the children would need a simple story at the time and a more complete story later on. Otherwise children spontaneously take responsibility for events over which they have no control and they come to believe they are powerless to choose their own directions in life. Tell your child in simple terms why that person left her and then help her work out her feelings. Make up stories together about someone like her dealing with just such a problem and work out how the story's heroine wins in the end. Stories that children can relate to will keep their interest and teach them valuable lessons.[21]

Pay special attention to feelings you have from when you were the age of your children. Ghost memories from childhood are aroused easily in the presence of children of a similar age and experience. If you were unhappy as a five-year-old, then your five-year-old child may trigger unhappy memories that arrive as feelings without words to identify their source. Stories you make from these feelings may uncover forgotten memories about your own childhood unhappiness. Be ready to welcome them into your life now, so they're not forced underground only to surface in some poorly timed way later on.

Sharing Ourselves

A special way to treasure our children is to share with them the feelings, beliefs, strengths, and faults that make us unique. We are not just Daddy or Mommy. We have a personal history that has already shaped who we are. Connect your experiences with theirs through stories of your childhood, then help them choose what to emulate and what to change. Here's a story my mother told my wife and sons on various occasions to keep the swelling of my head in check:

Once upon a time, a cocky five-year-old boy thought he was hot stuff, as five-year-olds do sometimes, and got careless about who he was rude to. He was walking his usual route past an elderly neighbor lady's home when his way was blocked momentarily by her large, slow-moving body. "Get out of my way, you big, fat, dog-doo lady," he said. This gentle neighbor was too shocked to answer but moved to let him pass. Later that day, Hot Stuff's mother brought him back to apologize and to learn a lesson he never forgot.

Our children need to experience us as people—separate from them—who choose to be parents. Our stories will help them to be more self-aware, too. The driving motivation for our children to accept our authority is their love and respect for us. Our relationship with them is one between precious human beings. It's a two-way street. We need to be real people for them and we want them to be real people with us. We owe them our best parenting and we want their cooperation in return.

Helping Our Children Help Us Stay in Control

Sharing ourselves means not only sharing our time but also sharing our love, our humor, our patience, and our values. With this in mind, another way we can share ourselves is to give our children authority to call us to account when we violate the values we teach them.

Kenny and Sarah clearly loved each other. That's why some of their friction became so painful. When she said, "You're a dumb daddy," she was saying in her six-year-old way that she knew he made mistakes. She was also inviting him to acknowledge this and to fix it. She wanted to forgive him. The door was wide open for Kenny to say, "You're right."

Marvelous benefits can come whenever we give our children permission to confront us when we go out of bounds. Admitting when we make a mistake and taking responsibility for it encourages our children to do the same. When our children catch us breaking our diet, smoking when we told them not to smoke, swearing when we agreed not to swear, or tracking mud into the house, we can thank them instead of getting angry or defensive by saying, "You're right. Thanks for helping me be the person I want to be."

In Margaret's case, her emotions were still so tightly tied to Joey's father that she frequently called Joey by his father's nickname. She didn't mean to offend Joey, but the ghost connections her mind created between Joey and his father were strong and largely outside of her awareness. When she recognized she was doing this, she agreed to stop and she gave Joey permission to call her on it if she slipped. Joey's resentments faded as he felt better able to stand up for himself.

Include Your Children in Your Daily Plans

Somehow, despite how busy you are, save *cheerful* energy for your children. I find it particularly sad to meet parents who missed their chances to enjoy their children. Too many career parents get caught up in their work and see their children for only minutes a day and on weekends. If parents this busy aren't very careful, they can become distracted by long to-do lists at home as well as at work. Sometimes children thrive while working alongside their mom or dad. If your children want you to participate in their activities, then you had best find the time or you'll miss out. Coming home exhausted from work every day cheats all of you out of your good time together. If you don't want to wake up years from now to realize your children's childhoods are gone, make it a priority to get involved now.

> **SUGGESTIONS FOR CHANGE.** Make good times at home a priority. Here are some ideas:
> - Come home from work with at least two hours of energy in reserve.
> - Give whoever takes care of the children all day private time in the evening.

- Do something loving with each member of the family every day, for example:
  - Ask about each person's day and really listen to what he or she tells you.
  - Compliment each family member individually.
  - Hug the kids who like physical contact.
  - Play games, read, or watch a favorite show together.
  - Help with homework.
  - Over time, bring home a special gift for each person.

Let's Do It Together

Sometimes the challenge of including children into a busy working schedule requires humor, imagination, and flexibility. The following two vignettes try to capture the spirit of loving good humor under stress with a preschooler and a teenager.

PRESCHOOL VERSION

Your preschooler invites you with pride to see what he did in your living room this morning while you were getting ready for work.

Preschooler: Daddy, I was busy! Come see what I did!
(The place is a shambles with the contents of the linen closet, desk, and toy boxes "organized" all over the room.)

You have a choice whether to respond in frustration or to affirm his excitement. Is your goal a clean house and a quick exit to work? Or is it celebrating his industry, creativity, and initiative and helping him learn how to time his projects better?

Daddy: Boy, have you been busy!
Preschooler: Yeah, I've been busy!

As best you can, you suspend judgment and irritation, because curiosity and affirmation serve your true interests better. Pursuing curiosity, you try to discover his motives.

> *Daddy:* You seem very pleased with yourself.
>
> *Preschooler:* Uh-huh.

What is going on in his little mind? How can you support his industry and channel it away from your frustration? The challenge is to celebrate his initiative, get the room cleaned up, and negotiate ways for him to play that don't add undue burden to your already overtaxing days.

> *Daddy:* This looks like some of the messes I make. Who do you suppose is going to clean this up?
>
> *Preschooler:* *(with a grin)* You!
>
> *Daddy:* What makes you think I will clean it up?
>
> *Preschooler:* That's your job.
>
> *Daddy:* Who told you that?
>
> *Preschooler:* Mommy said so. She tells you to clean up and you have to do it.
>
> *Daddy:* You are very good at listening to what Mommy says. And I think you are having a very good time trying to get me to do what you want me to do.
>
> *Preschooler:* Uh-huh.
>
> *Daddy:* Tell you what, I'll clean this up if you will tell me where everything goes.
>
> *Preschooler:* Okay!
>
> *(End of scene.)*

The dialogue takes maybe five minutes, cleaning up maybe another ten minutes, and you have fun with your child instead of a fight. During the cleanup, you might tell him he is not allowed to help—he can only direct you where to put things. This may last only briefly before he insists on helping, despite your mock protests. Try your best to enjoy the time with him. Finish the project together with smiles if possible and accept that you are now ten minutes late.

TEENAGE VERSION

Imagine your teenager asks for your help with her homework. She has a paper to write and can't think of what to write about. You sit down with her at the computer.

Mom:	What's the assignment?
Teenager:	We're supposed to write a two-page paper on any topic we want.
Mom:	What ideas do you have?
Teenager:	I haven't been able to think of anything.
Mom:	Well, what's of interest to you?
Teenager:	You come up with something. I can't think right now.
Mom:	Well, how about something in the news or something going on at school?
Teenager:	Mom, I'm tired. I think I'll do this tomorrow.
Mom:	When is it due?
Teenager:	Third period.
Mom:	Tomorrow?
Teenager:	Yes.
Mom:	Come on. I know you're tired, but I'll bet you'll feel less tired if we can get this thing done.
Teenager:	Well, you come up with something then.

So now what do you do? She has abdicated responsibility for the moment. How much help is a good idea? When does helping become doing it for her? What is the loving thing to do?

Mom:	How about something on family fighting?
Teenager:	You start.
Mom:	You want me to do this for you?
Teenager:	I need help getting started. I don't know what to do.
Mom:	Okay. Let's try something like . . .

It turns out this time that you coax a paper out of her that is at least 50 percent your words and 90 percent your energy. At times you need to go a long way in helping a discouraged student, especially in the beginning when she may feel most intimidated by her assignments. That's assuming you are even able to be of help with her assignment. Many of us realize our children are being taught subjects or information we never learned.

On those occasions when she is frustrated by work you also don't understand, you may need to be very supportive without being much help. Affirm her ability to figure it out, encourage her persistence, and empathize with her fatigue. Perhaps she can read her assignment to you as she tries to decipher what to do. Let her know that her efforts to learn are wonderful and important and they will eventually pay off. She can always approach her teacher or another student and try to figure it out tomorrow.

If she turns on you in frustration, don't take it too seriously. Be willing to give up gracefully when she makes it clear that that is what she wants you to do.

Teenager:	Mom, I just can't do this tonight. I'll ask the teacher for an extension tomorrow.
Mom:	Do you want my help tomorrow night?
Teenager:	I don't know.
Mom:	Okay, sounds like you need some sleep. We can talk about it tomorrow.
Teenager:	Thank you.

Mom: Love you.

Teenager: Good night.

If this becomes a recurrent scene, then you may have to look deeper. Is this subject something she has always struggled with and needs ongoing extra help with? Is she depressed or distracted by something else? At a better time ask how she's doing and what she thinks is making her studies difficult. Still stumped? Solicit her teacher's input or the school counselor's. If she still needs special help, ask your family doctor or a friend.

Yes, I Can Finish Cooking Later

Sometimes our children ambush us at inconvenient times. When that happens by chance, it is not usually much of a problem. Take a deep breath. Decide how quickly you can respond, and give a clear message when you will be available. If you're feeling frazzled, as you will from time to time, at least remember how precious your children are and try not to snap at them.

In general, if you want your children to respond quickly, model that speed yourself. Suspend what you're doing for the few moments it takes to find out what they need. Often a quick and timely response will avert more complicated and time-consuming confrontations later on. If you happen to be cooking, turn down the stove, help them find a satisfying activity, then go back to the stove. Let the decision about when meals are ready become a family decision. If others complain about a late meal, involve them in getting everything ready.

Sure, But I Need to Clean Up the Paint First

When you cannot respond right away, that too can be a helpful model for your children to learn patience and restraint. Briefly tell them why you cannot respond right away (they will be listening to learn ways to put you off), and tell them as specifically as you can how soon they can expect you.

Eight-year-old:	Daddy, we need you right now! Buddy and Angie are fighting!
Daddy:	Honey, I am right in the middle of painting the living room. Can it wait a few minutes?
Eight-year-old:	I'll go ask. *(She leaves briefly and returns.)* They won't stop fighting.
Daddy:	Okay, I'm coming. *(He puts down the wet paint roller and heads for the fight.)* Whoa! Who wants to help me paint the living room?
Buddy and Angie:	*(together)* I do, I do!
Daddy:	Okay, but you have to come now because the paint is wet and we don't want it to dry in the wrong place.

(The fighting stops and the new challenge emerges of superintending three novice room painters.)

Did the father in this example make a mistake? That's always a risk in parenting active children. But in this case any harm to the paint job was minor and readily fixed, unlike emotional assaults on a young child's soul, as can happen when a parent screams at a child not to step in the wet paint. Work collaboratively with your children so they will learn to work collaboratively with you. The quickest way to paint a room is not always the quickest way to develop your children's self-esteem and cooperation.

Priority #1 Is to Nourish Your Children's Personal Growth

After the painting was done, the quality of the job became a focus for productive discussions with the children about priorities in one's life and how people always have to balance caring against convenience.

As it turned out, the paint job took an extra six hours and ended with paint all over everyone. The reward (besides a clogged sink drain)? The children had a very good time and Mommy couldn't stop laughing when she got home and saw Daddy and three children covered in paint. It became a favorite family story.

Listening Is Caring

The best way to share with children (or adults) is to listen—with full, focused attention. Try to understand the obvious message as well as any unspoken message in what they are saying. Concentrate on the child who is speaking and keep an open mind. Listening is not just being quiet while someone talks and talks and you attend to something else. You are not really listening if you have one eye on the newspaper or the stove or the television or the baby.

One way to keep yourself honest is to paraphrase back what you hear your children say. Did you get it right? If not, then they try again and you try again.

The object is to leave them knowing that you know what they want you to know and that you feel what they want you to feel. The payoff is their enriched self-esteem and confidence as communicators. Your reward will be their willingness to tell you clearly what they need and how they feel—information you need to know to be a good parent. In addition, listening is one of the clearest and most effective ways to say to your children, "I love you, you are precious, and I really want to know who you are."

Listening to Understand

Sometimes hearing our children describe their lives requires a huge leap for us, especially when their experience is completely outside our own. Alienation develops over time if we fail to make these cross-generational leaps. By the time our children enter their late elementary school years and sometimes well before that they are living in environments we may know little about. We are outsiders to their realities as much as they are outsiders to ours.

Listening to understand means withholding judgment about what is and what should be and opening yourself to learn from your children. If you are a consistently good listener, they will seek you out to talk. Given the chance to be understood they will go to astonishing lengths to communicate. I once worked with a single mother and her three teenage girls. The teenagers regularly tried to engage their mother in conversations, but the mother was too preoccupied with her own lifelong burdens. She was literally unable at times to comprehend what her girls were saying to her. Nonetheless they knew she loved them because of the many other ways she shared her love, so they kept trying to talk with her.

When what we say repeatedly lacks empathy or conveys disrespect, some children will still go to extraordinary lengths to communicate—only with much greater risks attached—by running away, failing in school, getting pregnant, or attempting suicide.

Listening to understand means answering the question, How can I understand their behavior and respect their integrity? Our children have good reasons for doing what they do. Our challenge is to read their behaviors accurately. Their behaviors and attitudes are not random—they emerge from the interplay of their inborn abilities and the life they have known. If we must act to protect them from some unacceptable danger, we do it with the knowledge that they need our help, not our censure.

We don't blame them or shame them for getting caught up in drugs, becoming pregnant, riding with an intoxicated driver, spending time with friends who carry guns, or skipping school. But we do reserve the right as parents to act strongly to protect our children from danger. We take these behaviors seriously and make it clear to our teenagers that we will not stand by and watch them get hurt any further. We don't want teenage rebelliousness to end with a case of

AIDS or in a car wreck. If their attitude or behavior endangers their health or safety, then we move with appropriate urgency to get help for them through our family doctor, school counselor, local mental health center, religious mentor, or community crisis center.

Sharing ourselves by sharing our stories with our children creates a pattern of talking together. You'll know you're on the right track when they complain, "Dad (or Mom), we've heard that one already!" You can respond, "Okay, so now it's your turn. Tell me something I don't know about you." In this way, we keep up with their needs and wishes, and they ask for what they want. Not only do we have the pleasure of getting to know their budding minds, we get the love and respect that come from children who know they are well loved.

Chapter 15

TEACHING DISCIPLINE AND BUILDING SELF-ESTEEM

Children naturally like to please their parents. We may inadvertently train them to be disruptive, rude, and selfish, but they would rather cooperate. And disciplining children who want to please us is much easier than disciplining children who don't. As in so many things, we reap what we sow. If our children can like and respect themselves for cooperating with us, they will.

Jeanne and Kenny encountered many difficult times with their small children. Their legacy of separation, anger, frustration, and exhaustion deeply impacted the children's emotional equilibrium. Stevie, Jeanne's toddler, had frequent tantrums in response to his mother's temper outbursts. Sarah was often moody, especially around times she went from one parent to the other. Rusty watched Sarah closely, so when she was cranky, he would be the pleaser, and when she was cooperative, he would grab the spotlight with crankiness of his own. Kenny and Jeanne struggled to recognize these patterns. All too often they got angry with their children when the real problem was their own misplaced frustration.

One basic skill a good parent must master is *staying centered* in a loving and respectful emotional space that withstands the pressures of daily child rearing. A reliable sense of humor is an indispensable ally in maintaining a good-natured approach to your children. Ways to keep your children focused in positive activities will come with study and practice. If we keep our children's preciousness in clear focus and their discipline restrained and forgiving, then our children will thrive. They will learn self-assurance and the joy of cooperation.

Modeling the love, respect, and cooperation we want our children to adopt as their own is our best and surest strategy for teaching them how to live with others happily. If, on the other hand, we routinely act in ways we tell our children not to act, then they will rightly rebel.

Teaching young children to go off by themselves for a while when they become too upset can be very helpful and is easily modeled by telling your children when *you* are too upset and *you* are going to your room for a while to calm down. Spanking cheats you and your children out of many better ways to deal with unruly behaviors and usually signals both parental frustration and an absence of better ideas. I like "come-along" strategies where you guide your young children toward new activities with an arm around their shoulder and comforting words in their ear. These strategies can work with teenagers, too. Win-win techniques affirm their feelings as well as your love and redirect them into acceptable activities. If you are short on ideas for acceptable activities, brainstorm with your children. Take them to your local library and do some reading. One book on cooperative play ideas that I like is *The Cooperative Sports & Games Book* by Terry Orlick, which presents a variety of win-win games for two or more children ages three and up.[22] You can also subscribe to a parenting magazine, talk with other parents, and ask your children's teachers. Specific ideas for managing active children are available from many sources. (See appendix D.)

Do to Your Children What You Would Have Them Do to You

The Golden Rule makes a good foundation for healthy parenting. We have a chance to reshape our children's misbehavior if we can remember that the "little monster" who has wrecked our peace of mind today is also the most precious investment we have and not too different from who we used to be. Instead of responding to the outward provocation, respond to the underlying need that the provocative behavior expresses. For example, when our ten-year-old throws her books and coat on the floor as she comes in from school, we respond to her distress rather than her anger. As parents, if we can stay loving with our unruly children, then our job will go more smoothly.

A colleague introduced me to the "love sandwich." When we need to confront an unruly child (or spouse), we start and finish what we have to say with the words "I love you" and sandwich between these phrases a clear statement of what we are unhappy about and what we want done about it: "Curtis, I love you. Now you have to go for a time-out in your room until you are ready to clean up the trash you just threw all over the kitchen. And I love you."

Unless they are unable to do so, children will return the respect, support, and restraint they experience from us. If they are unable to reciprocate our love and patience, they may have problems that warrant professional evaluation. Nearly one in twenty American children are so distractible they are not able to stay focused and reliably finish what they start. Some children are depressed enough that they can't generate the energy or motivation to follow through with requested chores or schoolwork. Children who are bullied or mistreated may express their distress through provocative behaviors at home or school. Healthy children bounce back from upset and anger within minutes to hours. If problems persist over weeks or months, then suspect a deeper problem that may warrant professional help.

Life in families is so much mellower and more enjoyable when parents model the behavior they expect from their children. It is all right to put down your newspaper or saucepan or paintbrush or novel to help your child get something done when he wants to do it. If he pesters you for more time than you want to give him, look inward and see what personal needs *you* have that are going unmet. Perhaps you need more privacy—if you do, arrange to get it. Or perhaps you're upset about something—if you are, figure out what it is. We have legitimate grounds to expect cooperation only if we model cooperation.

Parents who routinely fail to respond quickly to their children have precious little right to complain when their children fail to respond quickly in return. Children learn by observing what we do. If we don't keep our promises, they learn it is not important to keep theirs.

The one-third of our children who are inherently more demanding are in special need of patient and loving parents. Some very active children require more direct and frequent supervision to keep them off the stovetop and out of the street. Moody children cry and fuss more quickly and require more soothing to calm down. Anxious children may cling to a parent and refuse to do things alone, even for brief moments. Parents must accept that these children need more time and energy in order to develop their self-care skills. They are sometimes called "difficult children" or "challenging children." Without the extra care they require, these children grow to create escalating difficulties for themselves and their families. With the extra love and attention they need, these children can become loving and creative adults with very interesting lives.

Impatience Speaks of Unmet Needs

If you repeatedly find yourself losing your temper with your children or with others, see it as a sign that you're overworked. It's time to take yourself aside and see what you need that you aren't getting. If you became irritable recently, something may be bothering you more than you realize. What was going on when you started feeling more on edge? As you think about this, do you get upset again? Talking with someone about it could help. Irritability, low energy, and loss of interest in usually pleasurable activities often mark depression. Do you need more private time away from your children? When was the last time you read a good book or took a long walk without someone demanding your attention? Is your marriage still happy? The longer you've been impatient, the more likely you will benefit from talking with a professional counselor for a while. If you're depressed or excessively anxious, see your doctor. If you're drinking too much, try AA and see your doctor. A chronically short temper hurts you and your family.

Respect Is a Two-Way Street

Respect is a two-way street right from the cradle. Our children's early experiences create the framework within which they build their relationships with other people. The way we treat our infants and small children stays with them throughout their lifetimes. The more that love, gentleness, steadiness, and praise dominate these early experiences, the more these qualities will weave themselves into the fabric of our children's personalities.

When we honor our children's uniqueness and separateness from us, they learn to honor us. Realize that even babies are people separate from us. Seek to know your children's individual sensitivities and let them make choices within the bounds of love and safety you set for them. If you use force with them, expect them to grow up believing that's how to treat others. Nurture and discipline them now in the ways you want them to treat you and others later on.

Help your children feel they live in a world that is friendly and loving so their ghost experiences are minimal and easily resolved as they grow.

Model Your Values

Teaching values to our children is as easy—and as difficult—as modeling them consistently in our own lives. They will copy what they experience with us. Children learn more from watching what we do than from hearing what we say. Show them it is okay to make mistakes, to accept their own mistakes with grace, and to take full responsibility for making amends by doing so yourself. For example, Germaine was able to apologize to Jeremy and to Paula for the excesses of his temper because he took full responsibility for his reactions. However, people who apologize for making the same mistakes over and over again invite dismissal for their hollow words. Kenny's empty promises to stop drinking lost him Jeanne's respect. She had to heal and believe in his healing before she could trust him again.

Jeanne also had fences to mend after her temper outbursts with Sarah and Stevie. Rebuilding a relationship that has been injured by humiliation and fear is like repairing a smoke-damaged home. It's a difficult, unpleasant, sometimes tedious process that requires effort, patience, and resources. Prevention is the better strategy.

Teach Assertiveness

The most straightforward way to teach our children to stand up for themselves is to stand up to them with a firm and loving discipline that makes room for their feelings and ideas while it holds them accountable for caring and respectful behavior. The key is for us to maintain these same standards in all of our interactions with them. They will emulate our behavior with a consistency similar to what we show them.

Rick related a story from his early teen years that illustrates a good way to deal with big trouble. He and Sonya, his year-younger sister, got caught up in a strip poker game with older teenagers who set it up so that Sonya lost. Some of the other boys put their hands on her bare body and she became frightened. Rick just looked on. His parents found out through neighbors who heard about it from their teenager, and Rick's parents were upset. Rick never learned what his parents said to Sonya, but they grounded him for a day in his room and held several long talks with him. He remembered that they never blamed him for what happened, even though most of the other boys were his friends. They didn't hold him responsible for his sister's choices. But they were very clear that the situation was absolutely unacceptable, that his sister could have been seriously harmed, and that criminal charges against some of his friends could have resulted had the situation gone just a little bit further. It was a lesson Rick clearly never forgot. His parents were patient, loving, understanding to a point, and very clear that what had happened was never to happen again.

Here's another illustration that came out of my work with Paula, Germaine, and Jeremy. The parents never lost their loving respect for Jeremy, but they firmly held him accountable for his own misbehavior.

Germaine:	Jeremy, I'm glad I didn't smack you, because I love you a lot, and I had enough of that with my dad. Where do you want us to go with this now?
Jeremy:	I guess I've got to pay the fine.
Germaine:	How do you propose to do that?
Jeremy:	I was hoping I could borrow it from you guys— then I'd pay it back as soon as I could.
Paula:	How soon is that? You don't have any regular source of income except your allowance, and that would take you a year if you paid me all of it.
Jeremy:	I can get odd jobs with my friends.
Germaine:	How about you sign a contract to pay us back $20 a week for fourteen weeks?
Jeremy:	That's more than $250.
Germaine:	You're quick. It's interest on the loan.
Jeremy:	That's not fair.
Paula:	Where else are you going to get that much money?
Jeremy:	I know guys who could steal it or sell crack to get it.
Paula:	Is that what you want to do?
Jeremy:	No.
Paula:	Then do we have a deal?
Jeremy:	Okay, okay. I'll do it.

Germaine:	And what if you fall behind on your payments? How about you put up your stereo as collateral?
Jeremy:	Now that's really no fair.
Paula:	Want to deal with a real loan shark instead?
Jeremy:	Oh, you guys are nasty!
Germaine:	Hey, we love you. We just don't want you getting the wrong idea about how the world really works out there.
Paula:	You have put us through a lot, you know. I for one need to know you're taking this thing seriously.
Jeremy:	All right. This is my problem. I'll take care of it. Now, can I have the $250?
Paula:	Who do I make the check out to?

Every member of the family is precious. We are all of equal value. What differs are the roles we play within the family. Our weather-beaten parental souls have acquired important wisdom for steering our families safely. We can therefore assert our senior rank in the business of taking care of our family while we also affirm the preciousness of our children.

Too Much Love Never Spoiled Anyone

Spoiled children are self-centered children. They haven't learned to value other people's feelings or to see themselves in a two-way relationship. Love is not the root of this problem. Failure to meet a child's basic need for love and emotional safety is the source of persistently spoiled behavior. Children need their parents to hold them to standards of civil and caring behavior; otherwise, the children lose respect for themselves, which shows up as low self-esteem and self-centered behavior. Emotional safety develops as parents reinforce caring behaviors and set firm limits on selfish behaviors. Loving behavior is learned over many interactions from birth onward and has at its core regard for other people. Spoiled behavior is manipulative—you'll recognize it by the resentment you feel when a spoiled child demands your attention. If you truly love your children, you will confront their self-centered manipulations and teach them to see how their behavior affects other people. Children become spoiled when their caregivers are afraid to hold them accountable for acting with love and respect. Love does not allow someone you really care about to get away with behaving selfishly.

Vince's father and mother both worked to keep up with the cost of housing, clothing, and feeding their three children. Eleven-year-old Vince had wheedled his parents out of many nice clothes and toys to show off to his friends. His mother, however, was learning to set better limits on his extortion. They were out shopping for groceries one day when Vince dragged her into a shoe store. He quickly spotted an expensive pair of sneakers.

Vince: Mom, all the other kids have cool sneakers. You have to get these for me.

Mother: Vince, we just bought you a new pair of sneakers two months ago.

Vince: Yeah, but Carl has these really neat new Nikes and I just have to have my own.

Mother: You know we can't afford shoes like this right now.

Vince: I don't care. Other kids will think we're poor and they won't play with me.

Mother: Vince, the answer is no. We don't have the money right now, and besides, you can't buy friends like that. If your friends are so into shoes that they won't play with you, then we have a very different problem.

Vince: Oh, there you go again, changing the subject. I want these shoes right now!

Mother: Vince, I said no. Now we're leaving. *(Vince starts crying loudly.)* That's not going to work, Vince. We're going home. Come with me right now, or you'll have to find your own way home.

(She leaves and Vince follows her.)

The irony of a confrontation like the one between Vince and his mother is that Vince and children like him come away from being firmly and fairly disciplined with a sense of calm that stems from knowing their parents can keep them in bounds. It's reassuring to children to know their parents are stronger than their own impulses. Children who act in self-centered ways to gain attention may be missing out on high-quality attention at home—attention that sometimes comes in the form of firm discipline.

Our undivided attention provides our children with basic emotional sustenance. They know they have our undivided attention when we say a firm and loving no and back it up. Even when they are brief, genuine messages of "I love you" can sweeten an entire day or a lifetime. Be on the lookout for these moments alone with your children. Find times to give them each your individual, undivided attention—while riding in the car, right after school, at bedtime, while doing the dishes, when helping with homework, when helping with their chores, and any other time when one of them wanders past alone.

Children who feel special like to cooperate. We can communicate our approval in frequent brief encounters if we will stay focused with our message: "I love you. You are special. You are beautiful. I'm all yours for right now. I love you."

When sibling rivalry shows up, deal with it directly. Say, "Yes, I love you—and I love your sister and brother, too. All of you are special. All of you are beautiful. I treasure my time with each of you. My heart has room for all of you." Attention focused individually on a child breathes confidence and self-esteem into his or her soul. Calling your children by name says you know who they are.

Meet Your Children 70 Percent of the Way

If you extend yourself well beyond halfway, you'll be surprised at how well your children learn to cooperate with you. Model consistent generosity to young children and they will grow generous in return. Especially when emotions become ragged, our willingness to meet our children well beyond halfway to find caring solutions will earn us special privileges in heaven and cooperation at home. If going more than halfway doesn't work, then we or our children are probably facing ghosts or a mental disorder.

When It's "My Way or the Highway," a Showdown Will Follow

Parents who want to overcontrol their children had better like to fight, because they will raise ready fighters or broken children. When children are told they must always behave just the way they are instructed, and when the instruction is to always stay within the lines, then their vitality is stifled and they will wilt or revolt. When we treat our children like we own them and they have no rights of their own, then we pretty much guarantee they will erupt in rage or implode with depression sometime in the future.

"Because I said so" is just not good enough for good parenting anymore. "Do it now and we'll talk about it later" can work, but only if the later discussion really happens. In parts of Europe in the eighteenth century, authorities on child rearing advocated that parents beat their children into obedience. Alice Miller unearthed quotes like this one from a German child-rearing authority: "Such disobedience amounts to a declaration of war against you. Your son is trying to usurp your authority, and you are justified in answering force with force. . . . The blows you administer should not be merely playful ones but should convince him that you are his master" (quoted from J. G. Kruger, *Some Thoughts on the Education of Children*, 1752). Alice Miller quotes from Rudolf Höss, the commandant of Auschwitz: "Whatever [my parents, teachers, and priests, and indeed . . . all grown-up people] said was always right. These principles by which I was brought up became second nature to me."[23] Seeing how authoritarian parenting strategies have contributed to authoritarian governments and horrible wars, we no longer tolerate such archaic treatment of children. Child beating is a criminal offense now. Still, not everyone has abandoned the practice of demeaning children, threatening them, or brutalizing them. When children are treated abusively, they and everyone else in the family suffer.

The vast majority of parents who become abusive were seriously maltreated during their own childhoods or lived in a family where someone else was maltreated. It is also common that the spouse or partner of an abusive parent grew up amidst abuse.

Unless tolerance for keeping violent secrets is unlearned and the family's secrets are fully aired, another generation will become infected with a similar tendency to abuse. Telling the story of your own experience with violence helps to lessen the grip these early experiences have on your future. If you fail to face these ghosts successfully, they may well blind you to the maltreatment others bring on your children or lead you to bring it on them yourself.

Children exposed to verbal assault can sustain serious emotional injury. When they finally decide not to take it anymore, they will stand up and fight their parents. Yelling, kicking walls, breaking things, hitting people, and injuring themselves become action strategies for telling their parents they no longer agree to obey. If parents respond in kind, the family may rupture with someone leaving or being ejected from the family. Sometimes the teenager is sent to live with a relative. Sometimes a spouse leaves with or without the children. When a member of your family chooses "the highway," you lose, too, both because a treasured member of the family is now missing and also because the tyranny persists.

Note: A child who yells, kicks walls, and throws long tantrums in a family where parents are consistently even-tempered and discipline is fair may well have a mental disorder and should be evaluated by a child psychiatrist or child psychologist.

We Get What We Give

The emotional logic of reciprocity is straightforward: loving parents beget loving children, and selfish parents beget selfish children. The difficulty is to see clearly what we are modeling and to realize that some of it comes back to haunt us through the creative genius of our children. They can be very good at playing our words and actions back to us. If you don't like their performances, you would do well to scrutinize your own. Who knows? Maybe you're treating yourself the same way you don't like your children treating you. In your frustration, do you say demeaning words to yourself and then chastise your child for saying rude words to you? We think our inner thoughts cannot be heard, but the attitudes our self-talk create become part of the family atmosphere we all live in. And those are attitudes you can do something about.

When in Doubt with Someone Vulnerable, Be Generous

Our children may do some outlandish testing of the expectations we set (likely throughout their short time with us until they leave home), especially as their strength of character develops, but the testing will not be malicious. It may become angry at times, but the bonds of caring will keep it from becoming vicious.

When our children become really hurtful, this is a wake-up call that some injury needs to be identified. Important information is missing, perhaps because the parties involved have given up trying to communicate. Try to focus on what is causing the pain. If you remain stuck, very likely either a major ghost or a mental disorder is present and undetected. Ask for help from a trusted friend, objective relative, or professional counselor.

When in Doubt with Someone Evil, Stay Away

Thomas Harris in *I'm OK, You're OK* describes a world-view common among people who grew up with early experiences of overwhelming fear, shame, or neglect. He names this perspective "I'm OK, you're not OK."[24] People who come to believe this way are convinced that the rest of the world is sick and owes them whatever they want. They readily become verbally and physically domineering and sometimes abusive or assaultive if others dare put up resistance. Dealing with such people presents a risk to your health. They are trapped by their inability to empathize with you, so you had best stay well away from them.

A growing number of studies of juvenile offenders are documenting the severe and sometimes catastrophic impact of early childhood trauma in setting the stage for later antisocial and criminal behavior. Children incarcerated for violent crimes almost universally report experiencing or witnessing violence against themselves or others. Children with these experiences are numbed to human violence and grow up to become adults with little regard for the feelings of others. The old term for them is "sociopaths." They can be charming, but they will take what they want by force if they can't get it in an easier way. When pressed, they will justify brutality or portray themselves as martyrs, warriors, or rescuers.[25]

Men and women become evil when they get caught up in the self-centeredness that comes from denying their own overwhelming emotional pain. It's better to leave such people alone. The price they are willing to extort from you can be continuous and exorbitant.

If you see sociopathy in someone in your family, all is not lost if you can convince that person to face his or her emotional pain instead of dumping it into the family. But your loved one will definitely need professional help. Say, "I love you. And I can't stand the way you use intimidation and force to get your way. You need help, even though you don't think you do. You have been injured over many years, but you can heal. You *can* face your own pain and shame and come away stronger, healthier, and a much better parent. You *deserve* to be treasured by those around you and to treasure yourself. If you continue to bully your way over the sensitivities of those who try to love you, you will never be sure of our love."

SUGGESTIONS FOR CHANGE. Choose a situation where you feel your child is frequently out of control regarding his or her behavior. For example, he or she might routinely argue rather than stop to think first. Now imagine that your child in this situation feels overwhelmed rather than willful or rebellious and is unable to cope rather than trying to give you a hard time. What different ideas come to mind to deal with him or her now? Think of ways to teach your child to ask for help or articulate confusion rather than argue: "You know, when I ask you to clean your room and you come up with arguments why you can't do it, I think you're trying to tell me something else altogether. Maybe you feel like I'm not spending enough time with you. Maybe you've reached the stage where a child is supposed to be embarrassed by anything a parent says. Whatever it is, I love you, and I think we can work out a better way than arguing all the time. What do you say?"

Chapter 16

PRIVACY — WE ALL NEED IT

One reality we all share is a need for time alone. People who were forced to live in shelters because of a natural disaster or homelessness will tell you that the extended loss of privacy makes these experiences highly stressful. The absence of adequate privacy is a major stumbling block for many couples and families. The protection of privacy in growing families requires healthy boundaries between people and healthy assertiveness in enforcing the boundaries. As parents we face potentially endless demands. Those of us who can protect some time for personal renewal will live happier lives. We will also do a better job of parenting, partnering, and holding a job.

Both adults and children need opportunities to be left alone. Denial of privacy in a family creates a pressure cooker that readily overheats. Marriages break up on the common shoals of unmet privacy needs. Violations of privacy sometimes lead to domestic violence or child abuse. Mutual respect for each other's modesty and autonomy are important aspects of caring for each other. Privacy needs are often hard to talk about and can be hard to grant in the heat of anger or the crush of family and work demands.

Be Your Own Person

Privacy for small children means giving them defined space and time they can control. Healthy parents set the limits of safety and acceptable behavior and allow their children to make choices within those boundaries. Very early on, children develop preferences about eating, sleeping, playing, and cuddling. Each affirmation of a child's choice reinforces his or her confidence in making other choices. Your ability to enjoy your children's exercise of these limited freedoms validates their joy and self-assurance.

As our children grow in size and character, their need for privacy also grows. Modesty is one form of privacy where we acknowledge that each child's body is hers or his alone, to be shared only as she or he chooses, again within the bounds of health and safety defined by the parents.

Some forms of privacy may seem more contentious. When your teenage son is on the phone with one of his friends, you do not have the absolute right to interrupt. After all, you don't want him telling you when you can talk with your friends.

Reciprocity means everyone lives by the same rules. If you need your teenager for some reason and he is on the phone, respect says to negotiate an agreement that both parties can live with. The more practice you and he have over the years in accomplishing these negotiations, the swifter and more fruitful they will be.

SUGGESTIONS FOR CHANGE. Sometimes intense negotiation will occur around privacy issues. In all of what you do, support your children in their attempts to become fully alive, curious, courageous, honest, assertive, competent, and caring. Then remind yourself that

- You're glad they have friends.
- You're glad they will stand up to you and voice a different opinion.
- You're glad you taught them mutual respect because they will negotiate an outcome that will meet your basic needs, too.

> Meanwhile, respect your children's privacy. That way when your son comes home from school demanding that you fix him something to eat and you are engrossed in an activity of your own, you can negotiate a time with him that allows you to complete what you're doing or invite him to fix a snack for himself.

Your Space Is Yours — Mine Is Mine

Likewise, let your daughter's room be her room so that your room can be your room. Her purse is her purse and yours is yours. In situations where living space is cramped, the rules of privacy are all the more important. All children need something to call their own. It might be a pillow or a stuffed animal. Respecting their privacy builds respect for their personhood and is essential for their growing self-esteem. They will reciprocate as they come to appreciate the privacy you grant them.

The right to personal privacy is also a fundamental barrier against abuse. Children from birth to adulthood have a right to a safe and healthy environment that promotes their optimal developmental and spiritual growth.

Privacy Issues Pervade Every Family Culture

Children can figure out by age four or five that behavior away from home follows different and more formal rules than behavior at home. You don't walk in on someone else in the bathroom at your friend's house, even though it may be okay with some members of your own family at home. These subtleties are well within the grasp of most small children. However, they need consistency so they know what the rules are in each place and they understand that the rules apply to parents as well as children. When I am taking a nap I do not want my six-year-old waking me up unless he really needs me. And he doesn't want me waking him up either.

Privacy is about freedom to choose what we want and what we don't want. Each of us gets to choose what happens with our own body and our own thoughts. The right of privacy grants us the right to choose how we spend at least some of our own time. It gives us a right to some space and some belongings that are our own. Every one of us has a right to privacy that emanates from the right to grow up in a family atmosphere of happiness, love, and understanding. The capacity of a family to grant privacy to its members represents a fundamental marker for that family's emotional health.

If I tell you I am too tired to figure out the fight we had earlier today, then my right to privacy gives me the right to postpone the discussion to a better time for me. Your right to privacy gives you the right to negotiate a time that is acceptable to you, too. Respect for each other's privacy communicates respect for each other. My right to privacy is my right to secure my own personal boundaries for physical and emotional safety and comfort.

The need for privacy derives directly from having a self and begins with the awareness of self. When a child discovers that the little hands he sees waving in front of him are under his own control, he has discovered his rudimentary self. Our sense of self is what defines us as individuals with unique names, attitudes, aptitudes, and style.

We have a need to be different enough from others so that we are recognizable as individual people. Imagine someone always calling you by some generic wrong name. Some people do this as an intentional affront.

Privacy rights belong to us at birth and grow as we grow. Healthy teenagers will struggle against us to emancipate themselves and define their own individuality. They will also honor our right to privacy and our right to be treated respectfully as their struggle progresses.

Mediation of privacy rights can get complex, but without privacy there is no meaningful respect or safety. Within a family culture where privacy is honored, everyone has a good chance to find happiness and spiritual fulfillment.

Consider Lucas, who decided at age twelve that he was tired of taking baths. He was now old enough, he said, to decide about his own hygiene, and a shower once a week was sufficient. So he began to shower just once a week and to do his laundry when he felt like it. Within several days his two sisters began to complain. By week's end his parents' embarrassment started to show. Two weeks into the experiment Lucas's mother said, "Enough." She wasn't going to tell Lucas how to take care of his body, but she was going to police the foul odors in the house. Spray cans of lemon-scented air freshener turned up in strategic places around the house and his sisters made liberal use of them. When Lucas complained, his mother suggested a family conference to discuss their disagreements. Lucas won his right to decide about his own body care and learned that privacy in a family means not intruding on others. How he smelled (or how loud he played his music) were matters involving others' privacy rights as well as his own.

Privacy is essential for our emotional health. Sometimes we get it by going away in our thoughts or imagination, other times we negotiate it with those we live with, and on occasion we simply take ourselves to a place where others can't find us. Within a family, parents must oversee the protection of privacy for children who are not yet equipped to protect themselves. Some children and adults need a great deal of privacy while others may need very little. Families must work out ways to grant appropriate opportunities for each member to be alone while also holding each member accountable for his or her participation in the family community.

Chapter 17

INSPIRING YOUR CHILDREN'S
IMAGINATIONS AND REACH

Healthy children create adventure. Their imaginations play at decoding the world they live in. They will try schemes of all kinds to master their expanding universe. Make-believe play helps children to develop essential skills—making friends, thinking ahead, negotiation, cooperation, problem solving, physical dexterity—and helps them to try on new roles.

Jeremy's imagination got ahead of his grip on real life in the drugstore. His shoplifting arrest gave him an enriched awareness of consequences. For the bargain price of his $250 fine and a trip to juvenile diversion court, he created the opportunity for a heart-to-heart family discussion about what they all most valued about living together.

In a Marathon, Carrots Are Better Than Sticks

The more support and opportunity children receive for constructive, creative adventure, the less parents will need to intervene to constrain unruly behaviors. This means giving extra parental time on the front end of their adventure planning. In child rearing, the rule is "pay me now or pay me later." Spend your time encouraging positive activities or you'll spend it undoing trouble later on. As they get used to creating their own dramas, your children will need less direction from you. Making time to help them create positive habits of play will make later discipline less necessary, less frequent, and less confrontational.

Children Would Rather Be Busy Than Bored

Healthy children readily join in a search for absorbing activity to keep their minds busy. When your children are bored enough, feeling neglected or lonely, or angry with you, they will find provocative ways to get your attention. What they do is more your choice than theirs.

Busy children need fewer constraints and raise fewer complaints. Keep their imaginations primed with constructive ideas for play and you will experience much less conflict with them.

> **SUGGESTIONS FOR CHANGE.** If your children have trouble avoiding boredom, take them to the library and ask the librarian for help finding idea books. Have your children make a list of different activities that each finds interesting. Help them take notes on how to make these activities work.

Dream and Believe in Possibilities

Beyond keeping our children busy, we can encourage them to use their imaginations to try out far-fetched ideas for the fun of it. There is no need to limit their ideas about what is possible—other than basic concerns for safety. Let them dream. In later discussions we can add our ideas about what reality allows in case our children haven't already figured this out for themselves. Healthy children have rich imaginations and many ideas about what they want. Even if their dreams seem unreachable to us, we can still support their explorations and enthusiasm.

Willy and Ariel were big dreamers. One day they built a spaceship out of chairs, blankets, and cardboard. When this version left too much to their imaginations, they found pictures of a space station in a magazine and using cardboard, wood, and paints created a life-size control module complete with computer terminal, CD music player, and kitchenette. They made spacesuits by wrapping themselves in tinfoil. Their space travel lasted off and on through several weeks.

Time will provide reality enough. Childhood is a time to imagine the impossible on the way to discovering the possible. Our children will be more fun and easier to live with if we can support these flights of fancy.

Try It!

Anytime a child asks if she can do something, you have a chance to encourage her initiative and confidence by telling her, "Try it!" If it is clearly dangerous, of course say no and help to define a safer alternative. Otherwise, offer to watch and to help if you're asked. She may accomplish something new. Then she can be proud, you can be proud, and her world will be enriched and expanded. Especially with your girls, give them encouragement to try new skills and ideas. Disturbing research shows consistent lower self-esteem for girls than for boys once they reach puberty as gender stereotypes and societal expectations erode their self-confidence.[26]

Sometimes your children will come up with really harebrained ideas without any awareness of the dangers involved. You may find yourself saying, "No, you cannot jump off the roof with your bat cape" or "No, you cannot drive alone before you get your driver's license."

The conversation need not end there. Suggest modifications to their plans to preserve the excitement yet reduce the danger. Perhaps there are enough leaves to be raked into a pile next to the roof so that young Batman could in fact try to fly safely. Or maybe you have mattresses around or some other approximation of a sensible landing spot. If driving alone is the thrill your daughter wants, then perhaps you could find a place off the road where she could take the wheel without breaking the law or her neck. If you routinely try to make these wishes come true for your children, they will reward you with appreciation and cooperation when it's your turn to ask for something.

When your children expect that your attitude toward their adventures will be supportive, then they will more readily consult you rather than sneak around you. They will be more willing to hear your ideas for the ways you may improve on their plans. Even rebellious teenagers will try to please their parents if to do so enhances their sense of competence and autonomy. On the other hand, if they learn there is no fun or satisfaction in sharing their plans with you, don't expect to hear from them.

We Might As Well Try to Control the Weather

We have never been, and will never be, completely in control of our children anymore than we can control the weather. In Seattle, where I live, the weather is notoriously unpredictable. People here keep their coats, hats, and umbrellas handy, ready for whatever the weather might bring. As parents, too, we can don our emotional coats, hats, and umbrellas when our children are having cold and rainy emotional days. For parents, good rest is like a good coat. Awareness of our children's moods is like a hat. A tough skin and good humor is like an umbrella. A clear conscience and a ghost-free relationship are like a good set of foul-weather gear and a reliable weather forecast. Equipped like this we are ready for anything.

Chapter 18

EXPECTING EXCELLENCE AND APPRECIATING WHAT YOU GET

The secret to instilling in our children a lasting standard of excellence is to combine an expectation of excellence with appreciation for whatever they actually do. When you always give them credit for what they have done, you encourage them to try again and continue to improve their performance. Expecting excellence from our children honors their dignity and shows them we care.

Every child's level of excellence is different. Setting expectations tailored to each child honors the child's individuality and shows that child we know who he or she really is. Excellence is not an absolute. If there were only one "best," we would live in a sterile world. The different levels of excellence allow each of us to strive toward new accomplishments. You may have a child who is musically talented, a pretty good soccer player, or clearly slower than most other children. Each child needs to find his or her own level of comfort and competence and pursue it for the pride that comes from setting a goal and reaching it. Let your children choose their own standards and they will keep striving to meet them. If you set goals for them that are truly beyond them, you will alienate them. If you show them they can do something that seemed unreachable, then you will boost their confidence and their willingness to try again.

A high-school student whose mother was a college English major discovered that her own love was physics and biology. She began as a freshman entering the local science competition and in her third year made it to the national competition. The goal was hers and her diligence amazed even her mother, who was immensely proud of her accomplishments.

An undersized and bookish boy was a member of the soccer team his father coached. His skills were mediocre, and through the season he became increasingly afraid of getting knocked down again. He hung back from the play on the field and became steadily more unhappy. When he asked his father if he could quit the team, his father told him, "You can't quit. Your friends will think you're a wimp. I won't have a quitter in my family." This dad needs some new skills and more imagination in helping his son to find what he likes and can be good at. If he really wants his son to play soccer, then he needs to help his son have fun, not bully him into eventual depression or revolt.

A physically talented girl decided to turn out for her first basketball team her freshman year in high school. During the first two practices she seemed unable to keep up with the other girls in the dribbling drills. In tears on the third day she asked her coach if she could quit for the day. Her coach saw her battered self-esteem and said, "Okay, see you tomorrow." At home she talked with her dad about quitting the team. Her dad reminded her it was her dream to play basketball. She returned to practice the next day and the next and steadily learned the game she'd never played before. By the end of her sophomore year she was a starter on the team and a confident young woman.

Do It Well and Reap the Satisfaction

The satisfaction we get from doing something comes from how much of ourselves we put into it and how well we believe it turns out. Encourage your children to risk trying their best. Learning good skills takes time and practice, but patience to keep working at it will pay off later in satisfaction and confidence. An effort that turns out well leaves us feeling good and ready for more.

If, on the other hand, you are someone who excels at criticizing yourself, then honor that, too. Recognize yourself for your skill in denying yourself. Appreciate how good you are at being negative about almost everything. From there you can start choosing to invest your energies in more positive thoughts and fairer assessments of yourself and probably your children as well. Consider cognitive behavioral therapy, which concentrates on identifying habitually negative thinking, correcting globally negative thoughts with more accurate statements, and practicing the use of honest self-talk. (See appendix D for suggestions for further reading.)

Work Hard to Build Your Self-Esteem

Hard work can be fun when the effort itself provides satisfaction. It helps if the work leads to a useful result, but the outcome is not crucial. A few years back following a huge snowstorm, I helped my dad and several friends dig our cars out of a snowdrift. We found the cars by finding the aerials buried in the snow. It took several hours to extract the cars so someone could drive them. That night another snowstorm reburied the cars. The effort of the first day when measured by outcome was wasted. However, we had a good time working together, and digging the cars out a second time had its humor and fun, too.

It takes courage to discover your best effort because you risk finding out the limits of your current skills. Ron was heartbroken for a while when he realized he was never going to beat his friend and neighbor in the 100-yard dash. They were close, but his neighbor always had the little extra speed he needed to win. A humbling challenge for any of us is to acknowledge that we have reached the limit of our ability. It is a sign of maturity and mental health to admit defeat gracefully when the contest is lost. It's a greater sign of health to be able to enjoy the contest regardless of who wins. When self-esteem becomes entangled with success, self-esteem too easily loses. It's okay to be the fastest runner in your class. It's also okay to be the slowest. Absolute speed or absolute ability is important in some frames of reference, but there are many different frames we can choose for our lives. Very few of our children (or us) are going to play in the National Basketball Association or become Fortune 500 executives. That's life. Thankfully, there are many different ways to find satisfaction in our lives. Help each of your children to choose a unique place in the family and in the world and to focus his or her efforts where that child finds genuine satisfaction.

Kenny worked on the line in a truck assembly plant, which hired him right out of the army. Shortly before the McGraths came to see me, the plant had reorganized into teams. At that time, Kenny expected to be chosen as a team leader because he was the most experienced person on the team. Instead, an older, quiet, and very steady man was chosen, even though he'd been at the plant only a year. Kenny went out and got drunk.

When he got home at 2 A.M., Jeanne cursed at him and shut him out of the bedroom. He slept on the sofa and the next day at work pretended everything was fine. He did what he was asked to do, ate lunch by himself, and went back to the bar after work. This went on for two weeks until one of his friends at work commented that he seemed down. Kenny denied it, but he went home instead of to the bar after work and went to sleep. Sarah was a year old then and even her crying at night didn't wake him up.

Over the next several months his drinking subsided, he regained his cheerfulness at work, and he and Jeanne got along better. He settled into a routine that included periodic binges on weekends, but he never missed work. Then the team leader had a heart attack. Kenny was asked to fill in for him. When the older man returned, he asked to step down, and Kenny kept the team leader job.

In the beginning Kenny believed his youth was the reason he wasn't chosen. But then he started noticing his own moodiness, irritability, and difficulty talking with other people. By watching the older man keep the team working together, he was able to set some new goals for himself and grow up a little. Kenny had misjudged his own readiness for leadership in the plant and felt cheated at first, but then he realized he was passed over fairly and for good reason. His new success was built on seeing himself as others saw him and making the difficult changes that prepared him to lead.

If You Never Fail, You Have Stopped Learning

Fear of failure is a major stumbling block on the road to excellence. Hiding behind the excuse "I didn't really try my hardest" is a surefire strategy for mediocrity. Recoveries from setbacks are like aerobic exercises for our self-esteem. Our resilience grows from knowing we can try and fail and still keep going. Admitting failure allows us to reassess what goals we have set and how we pursue them and helps us to improve our skills and strategies.

Trying and failing is the essence of good science and good parenting. As in science, failures can be great teachers. They tell us we didn't have the right idea after all or didn't pursue it in a way that worked. We need to reassess the situation, come up with a different approach, and try again. Children trained in this method of trial and error and then a new trial learn to keep looking for better ideas, rather than feeling discouraged or diminished by the ones that don't work out. The paths to great discoveries are littered with wrong answers. We don't get it right by being afraid to be wrong.

Give your best, expect their best, and accept the best you can do together for the time being. Then put your heads together and come up with new ideas about how to go forward. You may find that you're taking two steps forward and one step back, but you'll grow side by side with your children, sharing together the success that comes with the confidence to keep trying.

SUGGESTIONS FOR CHANGE. Remember a time you felt really challenged by something you were assigned to do. At an appropriate family time, tell your children about some of your efforts to excel and how they turned out. Tell them about winning and losing and how you handled those situations. If you remember being especially frustrated at any point, that could be an excellent lesson to share. How did you deal with your feelings? After times you lost, how did you recover to try again? Let your children know you understand how hard it can be to try your best and not meet expectations. And let them know that their value as a person never depends on any one task or assignment or endeavor. They can always regroup and find another path to personal fulfillment if they keep on trying.

STEP 5

ASK FOR HELP

Raising children is no job for loners. The more severe the problems in your family, the more you will benefit from calling on others for help.

PARENTING IS EXHAUSTING. There were times with my own kids when I yearned for someone to step in and rescue me and make everyone else leave me alone. In crisis moments we might be able to call on our partner, a family member, or a special friend. If no one responds, God help our children and us. Family pressures can generate a world of hurt. When your everyday sense of humor abandons you, it's time for either a break or a breakdown. Do yourself a favor—look at your unmet needs and get good help.

Step 5 focuses on getting help. You have good ideas about why your family is in trouble and you know your own strengths. Now it's time to find the help you and your family need. We'll start by looking at what else is available in the self-help market. This includes community resources, groups, and programs, as well as specialty books and videos.

Chapter 19

WHAT'S MISSING?

If the job of reclaiming your family from all the legacies, illnesses, bad temperaments, and cultural intrusions has sapped your energy, maybe you need a time-out or a vacation. Maybe you need new skills, adults to talk with, connection with family, or respite from hounding inner voices or demanding children. Whatever your needs, it's time to address them. Reach out to other people for companionship, new ideas, a helping hand, and new inspiration.

> **SUGGESTIONS FOR CHANGE.** Imagine you have one hour in which to do anything you want. What would you do? Who, if anyone, would you choose to do it with? Plan such an hour and make it happen. If you need to, get someone (a helping hand) to cover for you so you are completely free of family responsibilities. Plan another hour. Do it again. Turn it into a regular event.

A strategy with clear goals will make your search for help easier. The first step is to think about what kind of help you need. Start by making a specific list of the help you need now. Perhaps your list will include some of the following:

- Companionship
- Someone to listen

- Respite
- Play ideas
- Recreation
- Hobbies
- Discipline strategies
- Support group
- Individual counseling
- Couples counseling/mediation
- An Anonymous group
- Interest groups
- Special schools
- Spiritual community
- Information on possible mental disorders
- Professional evaluation

With list in hand, start researching resources in your own community. Good first calls may be to your local community information line or crisis clinic, your library information service, the United Way, the YMCA or YWCA, your local Parent-Teacher-Student Association, or a local church, synagogue, or mosque. Talk with your children's teachers. Try calling parents of your children's friends or classmates (the school office or PTSA may have the phone numbers). Invite people you know to meet for mutual support and problem solving. Post a flyer on a local bulletin board to call people together, or even place an advertisement in a local newspaper: "Parents with [your children's ages] children seek similarly overloaded parents for mutual encouragement, occasional problem solving, and shared humor."

All of this takes energy and organizing skills well within the reach of most parents. Just stay close to your comfort zone and ask others to do the rest. Insist that the meetings you host or attend include a time for fun and something to snack on.

Community groups will sometimes sponsor parenting classes, couples seminars, single-parent groups, or family nights. See what your own community offers. Ask a family member, friend, or neighbor to go with you to a class or event.

If someone in your family suffers from a particular mental disorder, perhaps you can join a support group. The Internet gives you access to enormous amounts of information about mental disorders (see listings in appendix C). You may be able to find a supportive chat room or support group, but be aware that there is highly variable quality control on these ventures at present.

Many communities have twelve-step programs, including Alcoholics Anonymous, Narcotics Anonymous, Overeaters Anonymous, Emotions Anonymous, and Adult Children of Alcoholics.

Self-Help Books

Many well-written self-help books are targeted to specific problems: depression, anxiety, alcoholic families, abuse, anger, living with someone with schizophrenia, Alzheimer's disease, autism, attention deficit hyperactivity disorder, marital problems, negotiating, divorce, stepfamilies, and more. They are available in good bookstores and online.

Center yourself with *Being Peace,* a wonderful short introduction to finding inner peace by the Vietnamese Buddhist monk Thich Nhat Hanh. Then read *Getting Past No* by William Ury, who will coach you on negotiating with your family to create family peace. Dr. Harold Koplewicz in *It's Nobody's Fault: New Hope and Help for Difficult Children and Their Parents* guides you in exploring the possibility your difficult child may have a mental disorder and perhaps you do, too. (You can find more information about these and other books in appendix D.)

Look for information and inspiration that fits your special needs. Be patient. Read as much as you can. In doing so you will clarify your needs, what help you can get on your own, and what help you need to seek elsewhere.

Chapter 20

SEEKING HELP

Mental disorders are not evidence of moral failure, but they require new choices and attitudes to ensure a good recovery. If self-help resources don't help you solve your family problems or if you have run out of energy trying to do it on your own, then tell your doctor, your rabbi, or your neighbor who works in mental health. Then if you still need help, seek the help of a psychiatrist, especially if you suspect a treatable mental disorder or problems just don't seem to be getting better with the help you already have.

Find Good Professional Help

When serious violations of interpersonal boundaries have occurred in your family background, including anyone having been raped, beaten, or repeatedly verbally humiliated, you will benefit from seeking professional help just as surely as if you had a fractured skull or a broken arm. How long it takes to heal depends on the extent of the injuries.

Actively addicted or suicidally depressed family members need professional help immediately. Look in the community services pages of your telephone book or ask your family doctor for local referral sources. I have included in appendix C the names and phone numbers for some of the national referral service hotlines. When you face your problems openly, your situation will improve.

Mental disorders warrant evaluation with a psychiatrist (with the title M.D. or D.O. after the doctor's name) because of the wide range of treatment approaches a psychiatrist commands, including medication. Alcohol and drug abuse treatments are now widely available in many communities and can be accessed by calling your local community information line, crisis clinic, doctor's office, or 911 operator. Competent psychiatric evaluation and sufficient follow-up will dramatically improve a family's quality of life in the face of these frequently devastating but very treatable mental disorders.

Clinical psychologists (with the title Ph.D. after their names) have developed highly effective talk therapies to deal with anxieties and mild-to-moderate depression, obsessions, anger, overeating, gambling, self-injury, and other problems with mood or impulse control. They also provide formal testing to characterize brain functioning, intelligence, learning problems, academic achievement, personality styles, and many mental conditions.

Counseling help for solving individual or family problems can be provided by counselors with a variety of training, including psychiatry (M.D. or D.O.), clinical psychology (Ph.D.), social work (A.C.S.W., M.S.W., L.C.S.W.), counseling (M.Ed., M.A., N.C.C., M.F.T., M.F.C.C.), nursing (R.N., A.R.N.P.), and others. Different states have different licensing requirements and different universities grant a variety of degrees, so the names of the various degrees and certificates may be different in your area. Doctoral degrees require from three to seven or more years of formal training after college. Master's degrees require one to two years of formal training after college. The more severe your family's problems, the better off you will be to hire someone with greater training and experience. Formal degrees tell you something about a person's self-discipline and years of training, but you will also want someone you like, who you feel comfortable talking with, and who has a grasp of the problems your family faces. The only sure way to evaluate these intangibles is to meet prospective counselors face to face.

Screen prospective counselors by telephone. Ask enough questions about your problems to get an idea of how they would approach them. Ask about their training and experience. Then set appointments with two or three potential counselors and make your own choice. You will probably be asked to pay for these sessions. Use them to learn more about your own problems and about the provider. Not every doctor or therapist will be competent—or sometimes even safe—to deal with your problems, so check out a prospective counselor's reputation by talking with other people. (See below, "Evaluating a Therapist.") You can learn if a counselor has been disciplined by checking with your state's appropriate professional quality assurance agency.

You are the consumer, which means when you contract with a doctor or counselor, you are the employer. Your money (or your insurance) pays our fees. We psychiatrists, psychologists, and counselors work for you. (This goes for your other doctors, too.) We are consultants to you and your family. You hire us, and you retain the final therapy decisions. You are obliged to pay for the time you schedule with us but only for the time you agree to.

Ask ahead of time if you have any questions about what charges are being generated. Some counselors offer reduced fees and occasionally will work without charge. Professional societies may have information about this for you. A number of religious organizations have counseling services also. Many of them offer sliding fee scales for families on limited incomes.

Talk therapy with a qualified counselor or psychotherapist can help you uproot your personal ghosts, retrain your brain in positive self-talk, and help you develop and pursue plans for better self-esteem. The difference between a counselor and a psychotherapist is that a counselor's job is to listen carefully and give helpful advice, whereas a psychotherapist's job is to listen carefully and then guide you toward solutions you come up with yourself. Psychotherapy offers deeper healing than counseling, requires a better-trained therapist, and takes more effort and time than counseling. Counseling can provide support and direction in parenting, getting along with your partner or spouse, and dealing with difficult life situations. When counseling doesn't seem to give enough help and relief, psychotherapy may be the best next step toward healing yourself.

What to Look for in a Psychotherapist

Seek psychotherapists who are well trained and happy in their own personal lives. Ask about how much time and in what kinds of programs they have trained and what experience they have had since they completed training. Ask if they are happily settled in a supportive relationship and if they have children the ages and sexes of your children.

It's very important to find someone with whom you have a good emotional fit. Meet with several candidates to get a feel for how they work. You want a person who understands your problems, has experience helping people like you, is comfortable to talk with, seems interested in helping you get better, answers your questions openly, and is affordable.

Going into psychotherapy by yourself is particularly useful for dealing with personal ghosts and other nagging conflicts in your life. The focus will be on ways to change your own bad habits that keep the conflicts alive. Usually this means remembering painful situations where you were not in control and figuring out how better to handle similar situations now. The more you perceived yourself to be the root of your problems growing up, the longer the therapy will be to reverse the distortions in your self-esteem.

Family therapy is my preferred way to deal with family problems because it gathers all the principal players in the conflicts and it brings together a powerful combination of resourceful people to help with healing. Small children can be amazingly helpful in bringing healing perspectives to the process. It's true that "children say the darndest things" and the things they say are often true and very enlightening. Children also bring wonderful energy to healing family wounds and tensions. Not every therapist is good at working with whole families, so ask about this before scheduling an appointment.

Formal group psychotherapy, led by a well-trained group leader, is a good setting for people wanting to work on issues arising from conflicts experienced growing up and other conflicts that are either "too hot to handle" with the people involved or when those people are not available for direct work. Group settings allow for more stimulation of ideas, both for choosing what to work on and for solutions. There is less individual attention, and fees tend to be lower. We can learn a great deal from watching other people struggle with their ghosts and genes, especially as we empathize with them and participate in helping them to find solutions. They, in turn, will help us. Friendships sometimes form out of these groups, but many group leaders discourage outside friendships while people are active members of the group in order to keep the group from splintering into cliques.

Professionally led couples and family groups are geared toward tougher family problems. These groups are harder to find. As with any therapist, pay attention to your intuitive feelings of safety. Do the group leaders seem to know what they're doing? Do they welcome everyone equally, or do they play favorites? Are the rules clear? Do group sessions start and end on time? Does everyone get comparable access to attention from the group? Do you retain the right to choose how you will participate, or are you pressured to do something you don't want to do? You are a free agent. Don't give away your right to say and do what you believe is right for you. Not all groups will fit you; find one that does.

Evaluating a Therapist

When it comes to evaluating a counselor, psychotherapist, or group leader, the first concern is always emotional safety. Trust your intuition about how safe you are emotionally with any therapist. Is your therapist mentally healthy? Does he or she seem to be a well-adjusted person or someone who is using your therapy to meet his or her own personal needs? The focus should be on you, not on the therapist. Therapists who share more about their own lives than you need to know for your own healing are taking advantage of you. Professional therapists keep clear boundaries about time, personal space, and respect for privacy. If you don't feel comfortable and trusting in your therapy, then you're likely in the wrong place for the work you need to do.

Here are a few basic questions to keep in mind in assessing a new therapist:

- Do you like the person? Are you comfortable in the therapist's office?
- Do you have any serious negative feelings toward the person?
- Does he or she listen well? Do you feel understood when you tell your story?
- Does the therapist help you frame your discussions so that you can approach your problems openly and constructively?
- Do sessions start and finish on time?
- Are the rules about touching clear and comfortable?
- Are personal confrontations guided toward mutual respect and appreciation of each other's dilemmas?
- Do you trust the person? If you are unsure, what happens when you talk about your mistrust?
- Periodically throughout the therapy ask the question, Am I getting better?

If boundaries in your therapy are not clear, safe, and respectful, you may find more hurt than help. Break off any therapy where you don't feel safe to talk about what you need to talk about without having someone pressure you for personal closeness. You alone define your own physical and emotional boundaries. You alone know your comfort zones. Discover them and enforce them, especially with people who are trying to help. If your therapist is not readily supportive of your personal boundaries, get out of that therapy and look for someone else. It is never appropriate for a professional counselor to become romantically or sexually involved with a client or patient.

It is normal in intensive psychotherapy for you to develop strong feelings toward your therapist. That is in fact how such therapy can help you the most. It becomes a safe place to explore how your feelings get tangled up with other people. Do you fall in love too quickly? Or mistrust people too much? Or always sabotage relationships when intimacy develops? Or get too angry with people you care about?

Strong feelings that create trouble in your life will arise with a good therapist in psychotherapy that is working. That is what makes psychotherapy so scary for some and so helpful when we work through these fears. We can choose to be ourselves with all our foibles in a safe and controlled setting where we can look at ourselves candidly and work out better ways to cope. Otherwise, we will keep making the same mistakes in uncontrolled settings like in our families and with our friends and coworkers.

Getting Started in Good Therapy Takes Time

You will earn your stripes as a patient. A good therapist should have a general working idea about how to help you within one to two hours of talking with you, especially if the problems are well defined at the start. Once the focal problems are defined, the work of psychotherapy will take more time the deeper and more longstanding the problems. A lifetime of habitually negative self-talk will take three months to a year or more in guided cognitive behavioral therapy for you to gain comfort with positively reframing your self-talk. Changing old patterns takes time and directed effort. Abuse issues take longer to heal because building trust takes time when your experience is that nobody is truly safe.

Family therapy takes several months to a year or more, also depending on how quickly bad habits are replaced by supportive and caring interactions. The quicker family members take responsibility for changing their individual behavior, the sooner esteem-enhancing relationships with each other can develop. Also in family settings there is a greater likelihood that someone has a mental disorder such as depression, anxiety, or alcohol abuse that needs to be addressed separately before peace is possible at home.

Maintaining Your Personal Leverage for Change

Your surest leverage for getting others to change comes from changing your own behavior. How you treat others is more important than how others treat you. For example, my problem is not that you are a bully but rather that I haven't figured out how to deal with you. My job is to figure out options I can carry out that will decrease your ability to bully me and increase my choices about what happens. When you wait for others to change, you put them in charge. Instead ask, "What can I do to make this situation better?" Now you are in charge of looking for options. Now you can use your creative imagination to try something you can control. If you don't succeed right away, no matter. You will have learned a lesson that will help refine what you try next.

Good luck in finding good help. Getting the right help is a significant part of successful healing. When I got lost in Moscow, the biggest part of finding my way home was finding the right train. The journey continued to be scary even after I got on the train because I didn't speak the language, I wasn't all that sure I was in fact on the right train, and I wasn't sure I would know when to get off, even if I was on the right train.

Knowing when to get off the psychotherapy train will come with doing good work. You will find yourself solving problems at home that before required your therapist's help. Maybe you'll begin to forget your therapy appointments because your needs are no longer so urgent. (Be aware that this also happens when your denial gets too strong.) Or maybe the train will break down and you'll decide to change trains or walk for a while.

You may need to be patient with a train that seems to be moving too slowly. Ask about it. Perhaps your therapist/conductor is aware of an oncoming train and you're off the main track for now until you deal with it and it passes safely by. When you're unsure about anything, ask direct questions. Good therapists have nothing to hide from you.

See appendix C for referral sources. If all else fails, send me a letter or an e-mail. I would love to hear from you, and there is a chance that if you ask the right questions in your message, you will figure out the answers before I respond.

SUGGESTIONS FOR CHANGE. Identify three areas where you could benefit from someone else's help. Then make a conscious decision about what you will do in each area—struggle alone a while longer, talk with a friend, seek a peer support situation, talk with your doctor or other professional, or choose another option.

STEP 6

FIND FRIENDS FOR YOURSELF
AND YOUR FAMILY

Involvement with other people who care

about you and share your values reinforces your healing,

strengthens your commitments to healthy family living,

and enriches the experience of parenthood.

HUMAN SURVIVAL RELIES on our ability to work together for common security. We humans have the longest period of helplessness as infants of any animals in the kingdom. Our capacity to work collectively generates the safety and resources required for our young to survive to an age and ability when they can fend for themselves.

It Takes a Village to Sustain a Family

All the complexities of parenting we have visited so far highlight the importance of trustworthy and caring adults at the foundation of a healthy family. It is virtually impossible for a healthy family to thrive in social isolation. Even an introvert ventures into the community when personal and family needs require. Sandra gathered up her courage to take herself and her two-year-old daughter to one more church in hopes of finding a place to belong. The welcome finally felt real. An usher introduced Sandra to the childcare coordinator, who showed her the toddler room and quickly engaged her daughter in doll play. The service spoke to her longing for companionship and spiritual nourishment. After the service, during which she had spent time away from her daughter for the first time in months, she felt refreshed and hopeful. Later she talked with the pastor, who seemed to understand what she said about her disabling depression and emotional pain that stemmed from a difficult childhood. She felt more at ease once she overcame her awkwardness with strangers and was rewarded with acceptance she had thought was out of reach. Her intractable loneliness loosened its familiar stranglehold on her soul.

Chapter 21

THE NEED FOR FRIENDS

Friends bring a wealth of possibility into our lives. We all benefit from friendships where we can have fun, speak our mind, share affection, work together, and help each other. Search for those special people and situations where you can share your pride and struggles and nourish your personal needs for love, friendship, recreation, intellectual challenge, and spiritual growth. Life with only your children or a partner can make you unduly dependent on them for meaning and cut you off from the stretching, tempering, exciting worlds that exist outside your family.

Social Isolation

Fears of unpleasant or intolerable social consequences cause many people to avoid social situations to the point of becoming housebound. Social phobias are remarkably common, characterized by a fear of groups or crowds that keeps us from going to the store or public gatherings. Fear of humiliation will keep us home so we won't have to face someone looking at us or the possibility we might have a panic attack in public. Shyness can make social conversation agonizing and awkward. Maybe your children regularly misbehave so you dread taking them to public places or your own irritability causes conflicts so you stay away from other people. Poverty, an accent, unusual physical or social characteristics, chronic fatigue, or simply being new to an area can all conspire to isolate a person. A jealous partner may deny you your right to socialize on your own. Confinements imposed in any of these ways can severely restrict our lives.

Nearly 10 percent of the U.S. population suffers from some form of anxiety that limits a person's activities. Significant discomfort in public or social settings should raise a question about whether you have a personal anxiety disorder. Social phobias (fear of groups larger than two or three), agoraphobia (fear of the marketplace or crowds), panic anxiety (sudden, overwhelming fear of dying or being humiliated), and generalized anxiety (fear from no apparent cause in many settings) are all potentially disabling disorders that can be substantially helped with cognitive behavioral therapy and/or appropriate medicines.

Depression can rob you of the motivation and energy to engage your friends and family or enjoy much of anything. So can heavy drinking or drug abuse. Maybe your only social contacts are with friends who drink or use drugs so you feel trapped either way. It can be painful to let go of old friends who persist with shaming, controlling, addictions, or abuse. Healing leads us out of confining relationships and into deeper new friendships and new associations.

Anxiety, depression, and substance abuse cripple many people who don't know these problems can be successfully treated with appropriate therapy and medication. (For help now, go back to chapter 20 and see appendix C.)

Solve the Trust Problem

Sustaining connections with safe and reliable people outside your immediate family is essential to healthy family living. It can also be a daunting problem. What if your track record in finding safe and reliable friends is a disaster? What do you do then?

SUGGESTIONS FOR CHANGE. The way out of this trap is the same one you used in Steps 1 and 2 to bring healing to your family, but this time the focus is on your own patterns of choosing whom to be close to. Search for the patterns that drive your current problem behaviors:

- What are the legacies (early painful experiences) that keep guiding you toward troublesome companions?
- How old were you when you learned to choose unreliable and unsafe friends?
- Who were the key people responsible for these early traumas in your life?

Write out your feelings and as many of the connections with these earlier painful experiences as you can. Once you identify these ghost legacies and what they do to intrude on your life now, you can make conscious choices that change the old patterns. Most likely you will need to face old fears of not being good enough for friends who are safe and loving or fears about coping without numbing yourself with a drug. It's up to you to see these connections and to unhook yourself from the past so you can connect with safe and caring people now.

Marcie's circle of friends organized their social life around smoking marijuana and drinking alcohol. They skipped class, got high together, and partied any weekend someone's parents were away. Marcie was finally suspended from school for truancy. Her parents then sent her to an inpatient drug and alcohol treatment program.

After completing the thirty-day program, Marcie was ready to give up smoking and drinking. She really did want to graduate from high school and go on to college. However, when she returned to school, her friends immediately invited her back into social drug use, so she had to choose. Her whole body said yes. She wanted the companionship and the wonderful feelings she got while high with her friends. But her brain told her no. She didn't want all the distractions, guilt feelings, and punishments that went with it—which meant she was going to be very much alone or she had to find a different group of friends. That's where her aftercare group came in. The people trying to help her escape the drug culture she was immersed in knew she needed a whole new social support system, including new friends and new ways to have fun. So her aftercare group became her friendship group for most of the next six months. She re-entered school with a new focus, studied with others, and joined the school newspaper staff. Slowly, new friendships formed and deepened. None of this was possible before her inpatient treatment, which helped her to redefine her goals, including school and friendships.

Safe and reliable people will be honest with you and will care enough to get angry if you offend them or hurt their feelings. They won't leave because of it and they won't become abusive, but they won't let injuries go unnoticed either. Reliable friends will keep their word. They will honor your right to make your own choices. For your part you will attract people who are like yourself. If you are unreliable, reliable friends will eventually choose other company.

If you are grieving over unresolved losses—a divorce, a death, an assault, a job loss, or the loss of your health—you are likely to feel more connected with people who share a similar experience and who deal with it the way you do. If you are not ready to deal with the voltage of your own pain, you might avoid people who are open about theirs. You might instead choose a relationship with someone whose denial and discomfort matches your own. The risk is that you support one another in unhealthy avoidance behaviors like taking drugs or overworking, or one of you learns to talk about feelings and the friendship falters because the other can't yet tolerate it. As you become more comfortable with your losses, you will want to talk about them more openly. If your friends are not ready, they will resist exposing themselves to pain they can't handle, perhaps to the point that your friendship suffers. With healthy friends you can negotiate ways to deal with painful feelings and reach agreements that serve you and the friendship.

Cling to Kindred Spirits

When you find a kindred spirit—someone you like who shares your sense of humor—treasure the friendship. Make it work in spite of your different tolerances for dealing with painful losses. The reason you keep losing friends may be your reluctance to face your own feelings about losses in your life and the low self-esteem that derives from these losses. Now might be a very good time to take a stand. Face the losses so the fear of losing someone doesn't keep you from making new friends. Face the emotional pain so your friendships grow stronger and more sustaining.

For the McGraths, one significant change for Kenny in the course of reconnecting with Jeanne was his decision to tell his boss about his drinking and marital problems. When Jeanne first threw him out of the house, he felt so humiliated and so depressed he couldn't talk with anyone. He wasn't on speaking terms with his own family. His coworkers intimidated him. The occasional conversation he struck up in the tavern would generate such angst that he sometimes threw up. So he suffered alone and drank alone to dull his anxiety.

After months of this his boss asked what was wrong. At first Kenny said he was fine, but later he decided to open up. The boss told

Kenny about Alcoholics Anonymous and helped him find a bowling league, where he met Jim, who was also separated from his family. Jim was attending AA and seeing a counselor through his church.

A while later Jim invited Kenny to join him in church. Kenny found himself crying as he watched young families in church together. He called me shortly thereafter to see if he could get back together with Jeanne.

Finding Companionship

Help for lonely people seeking companionship has been a growth industry in America for years. Counselors, singles clubs, religious groups, matchmakers—people spend and make a lot of money fighting loneliness. The question of how to make successful social connections can stump the best of us. So what's the secret? How do you find the love and friendship outside your family that can help you sustain a joyful, productive, spiritually satisfying lifestyle?

The "secret" is you have to work at it. Think about the people you already know. Who might you ask to spend time with? What might you do together that would likely mean a good time for both of you? Maybe you could go for a walk together or take the children to the zoo or take a bus to a nice spot away from your usual tensions. Choose someone you can feel at ease with—not a date and not a stand-in for one of your longstanding conflicts—such as an elderly person for whom you could provide companionship or another parent with problems like yours. You could also go to places where you can meet new people—public lectures, extension classes, a local health club, a walking group, or your child's school, for example. Perhaps volunteer at a local hospital or for a cause you believe in. That way you can meet new people and work side by side with them while a friendship grows.

How about a Dog or a Cat?

A surprisingly common solution to loneliness is to get a friendly dog or cat. Group Health Cooperative of Seattle asked their members what ideas were most helpful in reducing their levels of depression. The number one response was having a dog or cat. Dogs have the added advantage of taking you on walks and helping you meet your neighbors. They will also provide bundles of affection and a modicum of security.

Although cats are sometimes stereotyped as being independent and aloof, they can also be very affectionate and bring much joy to their human companions. (I've heard that some felines will even put up with being taken for walks!) And I can guarantee that a ferret on a leash will create opportunities for conversation.

Clearly, all pets require care, training, and attention, so this solution is not for everybody. Once you make the leap, remember that it takes time for a new pet to feel at home with you, just as it will take you time to feel at home with your pet. The Humane Society or your local animal shelter may have wonderful pets that are already house-trained and old enough not to chew up everything in sight.

Chapter 22

CARING TOGETHER

We grow spiritually and find greater happiness as we exercise our capacities to care about other people. The essence of good parenting is serving our children's true needs. We will know we are on the right track when our children grow in confidence, generosity, responsibility, humility, humor, and determination in relationships with their friends, neighbors, extended family, and us. Without a loving community in which to grow up, they will miss important opportunities to develop these essential skills and relationships.

Ordinarily, the first place to look for a caring community is our own extended family. Are there relatives who are healthy enough to listen and empathize? Maybe they've been through similar trials. If we assure them we are asking to be understood and not rescued, will they agree to listen? (They may fear becoming overwhelmed by our difficulties or their own.) Take the risk to reach out one more time. As you reach out, keep in mind that you want to remain responsible for your own healing, you want to understand the perspectives of those you reach out to, and you want to be explicit about any requests you make of them. That means listening to them as carefully as you need them to listen to you.

Religious Communities Are Ready-Made Places to Seek Support

For someone seeking a supportive community outside the family, religious communities could prove to be fertile places to seek personal and family sanctuary. They are widely available, often stable, resourceful, and accessible places where families are routinely welcomed. You might already have some connection through an acquaintance or previous experience. When you visit a new congregation, trust your intuition (hopefully ghost-free by now) about what feels safe and right. First impressions are important and will help you to make a good choice for yourself and your family. The same general guidelines for finding a good psychotherapist can be applied to finding a safe community.

Many religious communities create for their members the loving, inclusive environment that fosters the generosity we have talked about. So these are likely places for your family to seek a community that will love and accept you as you are.

The rituals that define religious groups can be perplexing and intimidating to newcomers, especially if you have little or no familiarity with them. Ask questions of people already in the community: What keeps them coming back? What meaning and nourishment do they find there? What opportunities are there to share with other parents and families?

Entering any community can be awkward for a newcomer. Steel yourself with a little extra courage and energy. Remember that you are on a search for a place that fits you. Visit a number of places to experience the warmth, energy, vision, and general comfort they offer. Then try one on for a while.

A search for community is not a test of your value as a human being. You are shopping for a good fit for who you and your family already are. You are choosing how to invest your heart and your time. Culture, ethnicity, doctrine, mission, economic status, and members' attitudes toward strangers all contribute to the atmosphere and general comfort of a new community.

Religious communities pray together. Prayer is a form of personal communication with the sources of power and meaning in our lives. For many religious people this source is God. Prayer, however, does not require a belief in God. Prayer can provide clarity, comfort, and direction through internally focused awareness and questioning. Religious groups pray in widely different ways, both in form and in the way prayer is directed. Keep in mind that we are always free to pray in our own ways, even in communities where prayer is formal and spoken together. Prayer is a special way of speaking to what is most important in our lives. It can be a discipline that renews our commitment to these beliefs. Meditation, quiet reflection, singing, and celebration can all be prayerful disciplines. What defines prayer

SUGGESTIONS FOR CHANGE. Look for a religious or cultural community that feels promising. Then ask questions that look below the surface.

- Do you like the people you meet?
- What beliefs and activities are most important to the community members?
- Where might you fit into the activities they pursue?
- What is the community's history?
- Does it have stable, respected leadership?

Shop around. You can find many wonderful groups if you look. Realistic expectations will help to lessen the distress of your search—look for a comfortable fit rather than a perfect fit. The more unfamiliar you are with religious traditions, the more different religious communities you may wish to visit before deciding. The same five questions above will help you in looking for a secular community.

is the search for connection with our fundamental values and the spirit of truth in the world.

Some religious communities are more traditional. Many Christian, Jewish, and Muslim communities have formal orders of worship (praying together with the whole community), which provide familiar rituals of remembrance, thanksgiving, repentance, personal comfort, spiritual renewal, and submission to God.

Other religious communities gather with outwardly less formal worship. The Society of Friends, for example, relies on personal discipline and preparation in coming together with heart and mind open to the Holy Spirit—the voice of God within each of us. My own chosen Anabaptist tradition combines a commitment to our individual relationship with God and spirit and community rituals to nourish our relationships with each other and with God within us.

Search out those congregations whose beliefs and activities speak to your soul and where you can have fun, speak your mind, share affection, work together, find support, and help other people.

A Mental Health Caution

I offer one caution about choosing a religious community: *Maintain your autonomy.* Don't give away your choices. Some communities demand obedience to authority that rests within the community. No human being is infallible; that is the realm of God alone. Communities also have ghosts, which means community decisions can be made based on outdated experience, bigotry, and all the other moral holes into which individuals fall. Religious authority has never been a guarantee against abuse of power. Wisdom tells us to keep our eyes open. If this reality is too scary to confront, you should look for spiritual community in other places. That will not, however, solve the quandary of abuse of power since it is an endemic possibility in any community. The solution is in recognizing abuse of power when it happens so you can protect yourself, avoid its impact, and enjoy the benefits that a healthy community can lavish on a family.

The mental health of a religious congregation can best be judged by the welcome it offers to strangers. The healthier a congregation, the more genuine its welcome to newcomers. The more you are expected to conform to predetermined beliefs, the more potential there is for exclusion over time. The notion "that you will go to hell if you don't believe as I do" is inherently unhealthy and evil. The notion is filled with ghost intrusions of abusive authority figures (see "When It's 'My Way or the Highway,' a Showdown Will Follow" in chapter 15) and historically has led to murder and war.

When religion serves emotional intolerance, inhumane actions masquerade as religious necessity. This is spiritual bankruptcy and a major potential pitfall for religious groups that organize around the failure of individuals to emancipate themselves from authoritarian parenting and to think and feel for themselves. Any of us who define ourselves against an enemy are at risk for projecting our own evil impulses onto that other person or group. During the McCarthy hearings of the U.S. House of Representatives Un-American Activities Committee in the early 1950s, authoritarian tactics were used to blacklist people who published positive words about Communism or were outspoken in criticizing American policies. It was common for Americans to brag about being "anti-Communist" as a way of saying "We're good people" without recognizing that they were acting in totalitarian ways themselves. The twin sins of arrogance and dehumanization lay the groundwork for evil and war.

Be aware that any human community may have an ugly underbelly. Safe communities acknowledge this, deal with it, and keep the potential for injuring each other an open topic for scrutiny. Self-righteous communities are always potentially harmful. Their judgment may someday wheel around to focus on you, and that will mark an unhappy chapter in your life.

Other Communities

Here's a list to stimulate your imagination and ingenuity about finding other possible communities.

- School-based organizations: PTSA, classroom volunteers
- Service activities: community, hospitals, neighborhood
- Interest groups: music, cars, computers, dance, exercise, science, reading, drama, crafts and hobbies
- Activity clubs: hiking, climbing, biking, bowling, gardening, walking
- Sports activities, community sports programs
- Political groups: candidates, initiatives, campaigns
- Advocacy groups: personal, community, global
- Support groups: childcare, alcohol/drug problems, depression, other mental disorders, health-related problems

The idea is to keep looking for ways to link up with other caring people. We need to plug into caring communities as much as lamps need to plug into electricity.

The more isolated and unsupported we are, the greater our need to take risks to find these communities. I hope the ideas I have shared throughout the book give you effective ways to break free of your fears and to find new energy. We are looking for a few good people to include in our lives—special people who appreciate our pride and struggles with our children. Our hope is to find at least one very special person who nourishes our personal needs for love, friendship, recreation, intellectual challenge, and spiritual growth.

Parenting Gets Overwhelming without Good Support

A central challenge for stressed parents is to stay calm, generous, and consistent. In the midst of family discord, we all need reliable people we can turn to for help. As we become isolated, our partners and our children too easily become our tormentors and we learn to hate them. These are times we most need to be raised up by our own village of supporters and placed gently on our feet again. Whom do we turn to? What if we don't have anybody right now?

You might need to start from scratch to build your social network. Breaking out of your isolation can be like jumping into a winter ocean—much to fear with little belief in the reward. Still, there is something about jumping into a cold ocean that tells us emphatically that we are *alive*. There is something exhilarating about surviving such an ordeal. It was freezing, but we did it!

Take a risk. Reach out to someone who might understand you.

Families flourish within communities that provide reliable, caring support. Friendship groups, neighborhood groups, social clubs, activity clubs, interest groups, recovery groups, religious communities, political groups, retreats, work-related groups, cooperatives, support groups—healthy families are part of multiple social networks for support and fulfillment. These connections provide invaluable reserves for renewal of family hope and rich opportunities to help other people.

Two stressed single mothers who band together will be richer for the partnership, even though no other new resources become immediately available between them. Companionship provides its own rewards. The key is learning to appreciate each other rather than restart a legacy war with a stand-in for some unfinished childhood relationship.

In caring communities we become important people to each other. We find friends to share our lives and families and our hopes and futures. We belong to a new extended "family" of our choosing where we add joy to the lives of other people as they add joy to ours.

Action Communities Empower Hope

The more powerfully a group benefits the lives of other people, the more it feeds the souls of its members. A potent way to overcome helplessness is to join with other people to change whatever makes us feel powerless. Mothers Against Drunk Driving (MADD), Mothers Against Violence in America (MAVIA), and Mothers for Police Accountability (MPA) are three powerful citizen-action groups created out of the rage and despair of their founders' maternal agonies.[27] Communal action provides companionship and a constructive outlet for our helplessness, rage, and pain.

Shared dilemmas create communities where our basic needs for friendship, love, and personal satisfaction can be met. This is the power of communal prayer and common action. Spirits rejuvenate when people meet for a common good.

Action in the Neighborhood

You can join in community with other people in so many ways. Let this list be a catalyst for your own search for healing connections with your neighbors.

- Shared childcare
- Neighborhood cleanup days
- A bake sale for a school or charity
- Tree-plantings in the community
- Visits to home- and hospital-bound neighbors
- Courtesy grocery shopping for shut-ins
- A community talent show
- Lobbying for traffic islands for a dangerous intersection
- Community food banks
- Political campaigning

Action in the Wider Community

You can find special joy in helping to solve larger community problems where you reap no immediate personal benefit other than making the world a better place for children now and in the future. Here are some issues in the community and the world that you might want to become involved in.

- Prevention of drunk driving
- Construction of a new park
- Literacy work (tutoring, collecting and distributing books)
- Teen health and teen pregnancy prevention
- Library services
- Crime prevention (including child-abuse prevention)
- Quality education
- Community activities for youth
- Preventive safety campaigns (seat belts, smoking cessation, bike helmets, gun safety, clean air and water)
- Disaster relief
- Environmental justice
- Abolition of weapons of mass destruction
- Abolition of war

The satisfaction that comes with helping others works like a grow light for our self-esteem. The stronger your self-esteem, the more patient and agile you will be in parenting your family successfully.

SUGGESTIONS FOR CHANGE. Make a commitment to reach out to other people. You will be renewed in the process of helping others. One way to start is to share this book with others and then invite them together to discuss it. Or develop one of the ideas above or one of your own. Commit to do *something*.

Finding other loving people to include in your life will follow naturally from the practice of gentleness and tenacity in your community activities. Good people abound who would love to share their lives and children with you if you are safe and caring, too.

A Note about Grandparents

Emotionally healthy grandparents bring profound blessings to our children and to us. A healthy relationship with them enriches the whole family. They respect our authority over their grandchildren and add stability, love, respite, and resources. When parents are un-available or disabled, grandparents sometimes parent their grand-children themselves.

On the other hand, intrusive and controlling grandparents model problems we are already too familiar with and need distance from. Set clear limits on their intrusiveness at the same time you celebrate their loving and respectful presence in your lives. "Josie, that child of yours just needs a good spanking." "Mom, don't tell me to spank my kids. And don't you spank them, either. Maybe you think it worked on us, but I will not have that for my children. I love you. I just have different ways I want to raise my kids than the ways you raised me." Encourage your parents to read this book, too. Maybe they will find a new home for their own ghosts.

Don't let their problems become a raw sore between you. Define acceptable ways to be together. Enforce the boundaries you set. Help them to see the mutual benefit in keeping clear lines of parental authority with your children.

Here's an example of how one parent set boundaries. Kathy's mother really wanted her grandchildren to grow up in the Catholic Church and made a comment about it every time they got together. Kathy had left the Catholic Church, and her husband, Bill, was Lutheran. They finally told her mother that she could take the chil-dren to Catholic services on any Sunday morning the children were with her as long as she agreed to let Kathy and Bill decide about the rest of the time.

Just as your parents' family was their domain, your family is your domain. You are in charge. Any uncertainty on your part or your par-ents' suggests unfinished business in your emancipation from them or their emancipation from you. Set loving limits with them that clearly define and value their appropriate grandparent roles. New possibilities, like tender shoots in springtime, will arise for renewed respect, affection, and mutual support.

Eight-year-old Dennis returned from a weekend with his grandparents as talkative as they'd ever seen him. His father, Allen, whose parents Dennis had been visiting, asked him how he liked his weekend. Dennis beamed and told about driving near the ocean with his grandfather in the old car. As his story unfolded it became clear that his grandfather had been driving quite fast. At one point Dennis showed fear as he talked about driving along the ocean cliffs, and he seemed to leave out a part of the story. His father asked, "What happened after you drove near the cliffs?" "Grandpa told me not to tell what happened." "So what happened?" "He got a ticket." "For speeding?" "Yes." "And for something else?" "Yes." "What else?" "They made him walk in a straight line, but he couldn't do it." "I'll have to talk with your grandfather about this." "Yeah, I thought that would happen."

Allen stopped by his parents' home later in the week and told his father he knew about the ticket. "I shouldn't have told Dennis not to tell." "No, that wasn't fair to him." "I'm sorry." "This is not a new problem, Dad." "It won't happen again. I lost my license for three months." "I hope you get the message this time. From now on, you have to promise me you will not drink when our kids come over or we won't be able to leave them with you." "I'm really sorry, Allen. Tell this to your mother, too, so she doesn't let me get away with it again."

Grandparents on the whole bring invaluable resources to a young family. The family connection with grandparents is irreplaceable. If it's broken and cannot be fixed, both sides lose. The effort to reconcile with your own estranged parents can repay you in multiple ways—your own relief, their renewal, their emotional support, their financial resources, their special relationships with your children, and their handing down of your family story to your children, just to name a few of the benefits. There is special strength in multigeneration families that makes the difficult job of parenting a little easier.

STEP 7

PURSUE SPIRITUAL HEALTH

Create meaning and energy for your family's

emotional and spiritual growth through

celebrating together life's exquisite preciousness.

SOONER OR LATER in parenting we are faced with the question, Why work so hard and sacrifice so much? The answer is, *Because we love each other.* That's what gives the whole enterprise meaning. When love recedes or fear and anger intervene, we face a spiritual crisis because we lose touch with what is most valuable in our lives.

Kenny faced such a crisis after Jeanne forced him to move out. For a while he lost all joy in living. His anger and dejection lasted more than a year until Sarah called him a "dumb daddy," which shocked him out of his denial. Affection for his family resurfaced and in time he realized that he needed to love himself as much as he loved Sarah and Rusty. He set a goal to treat both himself and his family with loving respect.

Step 7 is written for those of you who, like Kenny, have lost yourself in a world of dashed hopes and abandoned dreams. Where does an isolated, beleaguered parent turn for the energy to create family change? I hope to show you that the twin miracles of life and love—which are all around us, even in the dregs of commercialism, poverty, and war—are accessible if you only know where to look for them, and they are powerful sources of new motivation and creative energy. Change begins with learning to treasure your own life so you can reach your full potential as a parent and as a person. The next chapter invites you to awaken to the sounds and smells and laughter of life's ebullience. You can do this on your own with the suggestions provided. I extend these invitations to patients in my office when medicines don't work or their life circumstances bear down too heavily.

Your first order of business is to love yourself as unconditionally as you would love a newborn baby. This is a tall order, but if you don't genuinely cherish yourself, your love for your children will decay in the same compost heap you dump yourself into. Love says to us, *You are precious beyond measure.* Our challenge is to realize the many ways that this is true. The exquisite intricacy of human life is a gift to us. And with that gift we are given the energy we need to reclaim our lives.

Margaret Hazen had an artist's eye for beauty, but she had to learn to see herself and her children as beautiful. Her struggle began years ago when her father and older brothers would tease her relentlessly. First she was too thin, then she was too fat, then too curvaceous. She couldn't win with them and didn't realize it until she was already married to Michael, who teased her in the same manner. One of my early interventions with Margaret was to tell her that she was beautiful and precious in the eyes of God, and so was every other person on the planet. She cried when I said it. Then I asked her to start noticing the abundance of life around her. Life sprouts up everywhere, I said to her, and we are gifted with the senses, understanding, and ability to celebrate these riches. Her eyes came alive as we talked and she leaned over to really see the plant on my office table. "Incredible!" she whispered.

I urge parents to see, like children do, the little miracles of life that surround them every day. A dandelion, despite its capacity to frustrate your gardening, is an astounding display of beauty, vigor, and biological architecture. If human industry has destroyed your natural environs, use your memory and imagination to see dandelions galore or remember your own favorite place of beauty. Don't let dreariness invade your soul. Fight back with a vision in your mind's eye and a song in your heart about how wonderful life can be.

As you immerse yourself in the marvels around you, you will find motivation to better parent the miracles in your charge, and you will be inspired by dreams of a happy, loving family. Your ability to celebrate the life around you can refuel your commitment to healthy lives at home.

Pursue your dreams with enthusiasm and fair expectations. Say no when you've had enough. And keep breathing.

Chapter 23

BELONGING

Finding a place where we feel welcome is important. If you belong to a community that celebrates you, such as a religious group, celebrate your good fortune. If you don't belong to a community that welcomes and celebrates you, you may need to find one.

> Kenny and Jeanne felt intimidated for many months by the difficulties inherent in seeking a spiritual home for their family. They tried the church that Kenny's friend Jim attended, but the experience failed to inspire them. Jeanne summarized it for both of them: "I couldn't follow the service sometimes, and other times I was just bored. The people were nice, but I don't want to go back." While growing up, Jeanne had gone to church with her mother on a few occasions, but no one in her family had joined any organized religious community. She wanted more for her own family so she kept looking until she found a small church that "helped me feel alive again." The McGraths began to attend regularly for the fellowship and new energy all of them came to value each week.

The Search for Spiritual Community at Home

Healthy families replenish their life energy each time a family member brings home good feelings from encounters in the world beyond the family. Perhaps your preschooler drew a picture of a rainbow.

Your fifth grader found a "neat" spider. Your teenager found a new passion. You met a friend for lunch. Your spouse enjoyed a walk in the park. Share the good feelings of your day with each other. Tell about the handmade pottery you really liked in the window of a shop you passed and the warm smile a stranger flashed back at you.

Where our lives have not been naturally abundant, we can make them more so. Even if our chances were limited in childhood, we can take time now to intentionally savor the beauty and mystery in the shape of a bird or the miracle of our sleeping or bawling children. Even a disgusting housefly has an artistic beauty, symmetry, delicacy, and ability to fly that are astounding when you look closely. Bring the energy from your amazement at these marvels of life back into your family to refuel your collective efforts to heal.

If you cannot feel astonishment when you look closely at nature's intricacies, is there anywhere you feel energized by what's around you—a painting, a classic car, a beautiful man or woman, a favorite place in your mind? If your answer is no, perhaps you are depressed. Depression can steal our capacity to experience the pleasures of our kaleidoscopic world. We lose our sense of belonging and our sense of purpose. At its most terrifying depths, depression can even rob us of our will to live. Whether we are depressed because of a biological slump or devastating experiences, our recovery depends on reconnecting our human spirit with the life around us (and getting the professional help we may need if the depression persists).

Gods of Our Childhood

The role that our religious beliefs play in healing our families depends on how flexible and nurturing a faith we possess. The tragedies in some of our lives put to the test our beliefs in a loving God or a caring human community. We are understandably confused when God allows so much misery and destruction. In addition, religious intolerance and persecution have been the cause of horrendous human suffering throughout history.

Margaret Hazen was raised to believe in a God who validates the sacredness of human life, but her life and her illness took her on a detour of depression, delusions, and heartache. Her new medications gave her a fresh start. When she heard on television that African-American young men were twice as likely to graduate from high school if they were active in a church, she was inspired to give it a try. She wanted Joey to stay in school and she wanted companionship for herself, so she started going to church on Sunday mornings. Friendly men and women greeted her wherever she visited, giving her a renewed sense of hope and the energy to approach Joey with a choice.

Margaret: Joey, I want you to come to church with me.

Joey: Did I hear you right?

Margaret: Yes, I think you need some healthy other people in your life, and I know I do, too. I saw on television where teenage boys raised in a church were much more likely to stay out of trouble and finish high school. I think it's worth a try.

Joey: Church is boring and dumb.

Margaret: You can help me choose which church to go to. I just want you to keep an open mind while we look around. I won't force you to attend someplace you really don't want to be, but I think you owe it to yourself to give it a good effort. Do you have any friends who go to church?

Joey: Yeah, Chris and his family go all the time.

Margaret: How about we start there?

Joey: Alright.

We seek a spiritual community where we can share what is best in ourselves with other people. Many such communities are not formally religious. I know of community clubs, nonprofit groups, and business communities where caring about each other is central to living and working together. A community doesn't have to have a large number of people—a special friendship can be a healing community, as can a book group, sewing circle, scout troop, babysitting co-op, or neighborhood block watch. Check your local newspapers and bulletin boards for events and group meetings, and ask people you meet where they find resources that sustain them.

Germaine grew up on Army bases around the United States and attended Sunday school when his mother could find one. She would drop him off at church, then pick him up afterward. He often had a good time, but occasionally he felt lost among strangers. By the time he was in junior high school, he'd had enough and refused to go anymore. Neither of his parents attended church other than on Easter and Christmas, but they did read the Bible at home on special occasions. When Germaine left home for college, he stopped thinking about church.

Paula grew up in a secular Jewish household that observed Rosh Hashanah and Yom Kippur but otherwise found community through the university where her father taught and the local school where her mother taught. Paula involved herself in Campfire Girls, a local chorus, dance classes, and sports, which kept her parents busy, too.

While Paula was still in medical school, the Durrens' schedule was too cramped and exhausting for them to think about joining any religious group. It wasn't until the children reached school age that a voice in Germaine's head started urging him to introduce their children to religion, which would bring moral education for Jeremy and Tawnia into focus. He and Paula held their first serious discussion about blending Judaism and Christianity for their children. Finding common ground took some deliberation, but they agreed that they wanted their children to learn about both traditions and be able to live comfortably in the Christian and Jewish communities. In time they decided to celebrate both Jewish and Christian holidays and to read the Bible together from time to time but not to involve themselves in a church or synagogue.

Instead, the Durrens became active members of the local soccer club that sponsored the teams Jeremy and Tawnia played on, and they became involved in school-related activities including fundraisers, school outings, a school drama program, and recruiting and training of classroom aides. Paula eventually became president of the local Parent-Teacher-Student Association and helped start a health clinic in Jeremy's high school.

The secret to creating an atmosphere of happiness, love, and understanding in your own home is to establish goals for your family that involve doing meaningful work for family members and others. Your reward will be knowing you helped another to live more fully. Figuring out how to do this consistently is a spiritual journey that leads us closer to inner peace and loving relationships.

Spiritual journeys do not necessarily require adherence to formal religious practices. For example, core teachings in Alcoholics Anonymous call on believers to rely on a Higher Power for strength and unshakable personal companionship. But AA can work for skeptics, too, if they're willing to look beyond the language and respond to the call to responsibility and community.

Kenny had a hard time with AA at first. Besides his own reluctance to admit his alcoholism, he wasn't comfortable with all the "God talk." However, he liked the fellowship and the religious aspect wasn't forced on him, so he stuck it out. Over time he became an active member of the group, made a few friends, and found it much easier to stay sober when he followed the program.

Life's abundance moves in and around us constantly. My invitation to you is to see life's treasure in everything. When you revere the vital and beautiful in your daily life, your children will also grow generous and reverent. And taking care of the natural abundance around you will help ensure that it will remain available to nourish future generations, too.

SUGGESTIONS FOR CHANGE. Take yourself (and your family, if they are willing) to a garden or park where peaceful meditation is possible. Sit quietly and notice the details of the leaves, the trees, the birds at play, the sounds of the wind. Speak your dreams for yourself and your family out loud or silently. Relax into the peace that surrounds you. And remember this experience. Carry it with you and replay it whenever you need to restore your hope and your energy for carrying on.

Our Common Humanity

We are all part of the boundless diversity of humankind. On a cosmic scale, any one of us is tiny and fragile, yet each of us embodies the miracle of creation. The more clearly we understand this, the less likely we will be to lose our tempers with our children or our neighbors. In their turn, they will be more tolerant of our momentary lapses and find it easier to resist any impulse to retaliate. As Kenny came to understand, we don't have all that much time to cherish each other.

Celebrate Life, Beauty, and Becoming

Today is a beautiful, blue-sky winter day in Seattle. The mountains are shining with new snow. The air is brisk. The sun is low and brilliant, and early morning frost crystals sparkle in the grass and on the bare branches. A spectacular winter day beckons my spirit.

More often it rains here. The silver grays; deep, wet browns; and soggy greens are magical in different ways. Rainy weather is still spectacular and renews my soul when I pause to see it and take it in: Spring shoots coming up. Daffodils about to bud. Camellias blooming pink on green. Flowering plum petals on my sodden deck.

Healthy children are spontaneously filled with wonder at all the new and curious things they see around them. Whenever your children marvel at something they discover, encourage their wonder and share in it. Seen through the eyes of children, our place in the world can seem at once terrifying and fascinating. Sharing with each other makes monumental problems seem smaller. Life becomes cruel only if we lose our connections with the miracle of being alive and sharing with others. Anne Frank taught us that even amidst the unholiest of evil, the family that shares a reverence for life can maintain their human dignity.

A Multitude of Opportunities to Renew Ourselves

The little moments when we celebrate life are important. They are the way we replenish our energy for trying to parent just a little bit better. For every ounce of energy we put out we must take in a new ounce or we will eventually exhaust ourselves. There is no lack of beauty to draw from—either out in the world or within our own imagination. Our job is to see it, feel it, smell it, taste it, hear it, sense it, imagine it, believe it. Replenishing our store of good feelings is a shared family responsibility. Everyone must put back into the family coffers of good energy enough love, forgiveness, cheer, humility, and graciousness for the family to successfully nurture the emotional and spiritual growth of all its members.

Little Robbie loved to draw cars. He'd find one he liked in the newspaper or a magazine and spend hours in his room drawing it. It was his way to escape from the tension and sadness that had filled his house every day since his grandmother died in a car wreck nearly a year ago. She had lived with Robbie and his parents as long as he could remember, and he was already six. When he came out of his room for dinner, he would show his parents his drawings. They would smile and hug and praise him for his pictures, and that made him feel warm inside. He felt he was making them happy, too. It was his way of saying, "Don't be sad anymore."

With all family members contributing what they can, there are usually enough reserves when someone needs to draw out more than he or she returns for a while. If the family reserves run dry, it's time to seek outside sources of support and renewal.

Robbie's mom told me how much his drawings and his eagerness to make her feel better really did make her feel better and made it easier to deal with the loss of her mother.

Goodness Is a Choice

Loving each other provides us one of the consummate satisfactions we can know in life. Another satisfaction, born of rage, is wielding unrestricted power. Our lives are split—good against evil. Parents are perfectly situated to become tyrants and torturers. Some do. All of us are capable of it. In this book you are learning ways that will help you choose good over evil, life over death, love over humiliation, celebration over desecration. The decisions fall to each one of us individually, within our own hearts.

The story, however, does not end there. Each of us contributes to the communities in which we live. If we are good neighbors, then we contribute to a community spirit of hospitality and cooperation. If we are rude, then we diminish the hospitality around us and spread dissension. As parents, we are the guardians of the future that our children will live out. The legacies we create for them help to shape attitudes and actions that they will carry into their communities as they become the next generation. Childhood scars on the souls of our community leaders and business leaders distort the decisions of these men and women in the same ways we have seen parental decisions become distorted, and the spirit of those decisions ripples throughout the community.

Healthy Spirituality Is Fundamental to Mental Health

The essence of healthy spirituality is to know that every one of us is a beautiful, lovable, precious child of Creation. Out of this knowledge we are able to accept and value others and ourselves. Bad things always happen when we fail to recognize each other's inherent worth.

The Bigger Picture

To love someone is to commit fully to that person's spiritual well-being. Perhaps at no time in our lives is this easier than when we hold our own newborn child. The wonder and humility that infuse our love for our children help us to limit our self-absorption and to see ourselves in life's bigger picture. Erik Erikson in *Childhood and Society* describes this ability to see that we are but a small part of the ongoing human adventure as a developmental milestone for adults. During this stage of our lives, which he calls "generativity," we invest ourselves "in establishing and guiding the next generation" toward creative, productive, and altruistic lives that enhance the welfare of the entire community.[28]

The critical time to foster mental health for a lifetime is the first six years of a child's life. Clearly, the earlier and more consistently we treasure a child, the more likely that child will grow up to be a good neighbor. Enormous resources are squandered around the world trying to protect communities from people with ravaged childhoods. If we could guarantee throughout the first six years of life that every child is loved, well fed, and protected from the overwhelming fears of abuse or neglect or war, we could save billions of dollars every year and the world's quality of life would be monumentally enhanced.

Dedication to healthy children can start right here with you and me. My challenge to you is to recognize the spiritual grace within you—your love of life—and to follow it.

SUGGESTIONS FOR CHANGE. Once you achieve a family atmosphere of happiness, love, and understanding, consider ways your family can reach out to others in need of the hope you have discovered. How can you and your children give to the neighborhood where you live, to the schools and workplaces where you spend your days, and to those on the margins of your town or city? Your lives will be even richer when you share your good fortune.

STEP 8

REFUSE TO GIVE UP

Rely on your own best judgment about what to try next, and seek help from others you trust. Find the love and stamina you need and you will bring happiness to your family.

BY NOW YOU know there is no easy road to recovery. Getting this far has no doubt been difficult, but I hope it has been inspiring. Nothing that builds up our human spirit is ever easy. Hard work directed carefully toward building mutual caring in our families fulfills a basic goal in our lives and nourishes our self-respect.

We've addressed despair a number of times and made suggestions for overcoming it. Here are a few final thoughts about hanging on and finding new approaches to old problems. The first part of chapter 24 shares the wonderful work of the Harvard Negotiation Project and William Ury's development of those ideas for building cooperation out of confrontation. These ideas have been more valuable to me and my patients than any other single resource in helping them to work through seemingly unsolvable differences. I then share the story of one beleaguered but indomitable mother who survived cancer, severe depression, and a divorce during her lowest days and has gone on to find happiness in life with her two teenage daughters. The message is simple: With courage and determination you, too, can resolve your family's longstanding problems and help create the family atmosphere of happiness, love, and understanding that the UN Rights of the Child Convention calls us to do.

Chapter 24

WHAT TO DO WHEN
RESISTANCE PERSISTS

William Ury, cofounder of the Harvard Negotiation Project, has developed a five-step strategy for breaking through stuck negotiations. Below is a very brief summary of these steps as presented in *Getting Past No: Negotiating Your Way from Confrontation to Cooperation,*[29] with an example I added. Success in difficult negotiations is often in the details as well as the follow-through, so if your initial efforts to use this abbreviated version of Ury's program fail, buy his book and read it thoroughly. You will very likely find the help you need to succeed.

The five steps are as follows:

1. **Don't react—step above the scene in your head.**
   Your three-year-old son runs to you sobbing that his six-year-old sister took his favorite blanket, and your daughter tearfully tells you her little brother came into her room and destroyed her drawing. Don't react and certainly don't take sides. Step back and take a deep breath. Try to imagine a way to soothe both children's hurt feelings. If you're already caught up in your own anger, frustration, or protectiveness, take a time-out by going in your imagination to a place well above the fracas where you can think about it from a distance before you choose your response.

2. **Don't argue—join the other's perspective.**
   Here's your chance to listen and to empathize with each side. Tell both children you want to hear them out, one at a time.

Maybe start with the one who approached you first: "Now slow down and tell me again what happened." Listen patiently and try to see the situation through each child's eyes. "I can see why you would feel angry when that happened." Don't argue with either of them. If either child objects while you seem to be siding with the other, reassure them that each in turn will have your undivided attention.

3. **Don't reject — reframe.**

    Don't tell either one he or she is wrong or argue with the stories the children tell you. Instead, listen carefully then put your own slant on the events they describe. Say to your three-year-old, "You got lonely, didn't you, and went into your sister's room to play with her. And when she told you to get lost you felt hurt and angry and you stomped on her drawing. Am I right?" Then say to your six-year-old, "You were working so hard on your drawing and your little brother came barging in right when you were in the middle of it and he wouldn't wait until you were finished. Then when he stomped on your picture you got furious and grabbed his blanket away from him. Am I right?" Now both children have a new way to look at what happened and you still haven't taken sides.

4. **Don't push — build the other an easy way to join you.**

    Offer a forum for the children to settle their differences. "What do you each think would be a fair way to end this situation?" Listen again to both sides. Let them decide between themselves what to do next. Add your own ideas if theirs don't seem acceptable: "Sammy, what if you tell your sister you're sorry you hurt her drawing and that you just wanted her to play with you and see if she will give you your blanket back?" "Julie, what if you tell Sammy you're sorry you couldn't play with him right away, but you were in the middle of a very important drawing and you're sorry you got angry with him, but he needs to let you finish what you're doing?" "You know, I was planning to take the two of you to the park this afternoon. Would you like that? If so, it's time to settle this and move on." If these initial offerings don't resolve the conflict, go back to earlier steps and listen for other conflicts that keep this one going.

5. **Don't escalate.**

    Use your power to educate about the consequences of continued confrontation and the benefits of agreement.

    For disputes that do not resolve themselves through the first four steps, you may need to spell out what's likely to happen: "If you two insist on fighting with each other, you will both be angry for a long time. The next time Sammy wants to play or Julie wants to draw, the other one isn't going to cooperate and we'll be right back here again. If you can work out how to play together when both of you want to and leave each other alone when that's what either of you wants, then you can both play together and do your special projects." If the children need time-outs or other consequences to increase their incentive to cooperate, now would be the time: "I think I'll take the blanket and the drawing materials and just hold them until the two of you figure out how to get along." "But that's not fair." "So work something out between you." "But he'll just come in my room and wreck my stuff again." "Not if he knows that you are available to play with him once in a while."

These five steps were worked out through many rigorous negotiating sessions in a wide variety of settings. If you truly adhere to them, they will work. In those instances where you can't seem to negotiate an agreement, go back to an earlier step and try again to build the bridges that allow you to work together. From the beginning, be sure you separate the people from the problem. In our example above, Sammy is not Julie's problem or vice versa; rather, Sammy's intrusion and his aggression are Julie's problem. For Sammy, it's Julie's refusal to play with him that's the problem, not Julie herself. Julie needs her work space and work time protected from intrusions that disrupt her concentration. Sammy needs someone to play with. The next step is to find a way that both their needs are met. That's what their mom did so well above. The key to finding win-win solutions is to stay with a creative thinking process until an idea finally emerges that works for all sides. That's why this process can sometimes take a long time. But it very seldom fails.

SUGGESTIONS FOR CHANGE. Here's a chance to integrate a number of skills we've worked on throughout the book. Choose a conflict that is central to the difficulties your family faces all the time. As an example, let's say that your spouse and your six-year-old usually end up in a screaming match, which you jump into to protect your child, only to infuriate your spouse. Get together for a family meeting. Focus on the conflict you have chosen and take yourselves through the five steps of *Getting Past No:* (1) step above the conflict, (2) join the other's point of view, (3) reframe the problem, (4) build a bridge between the opposing sides, and (5) educate about the consequences of continuing to fight and the benefits of cooperation. Any time the process doesn't work, go back and take a different approach to each step until you get a real agreement.

A Courageous Woman

Five years ago, Sharon was married to a successful attorney, living on a six-figure income in a beautiful suburban house, raising two beautiful if sometimes challenging preteen daughters, and enjoying her own career as a nurse practitioner in a small inner-city healthcare clinic. Then she was diagnosed with breast cancer. Sharon's fear of cancer unnerved her. She couldn't sit still at the dinner table and wasn't able to converse without bursting into tears.

Her husband, Ron, had been relying on her to run the household while he managed his law firm. The added stress caused old arguments to erupt, and the tensions at home became unbearable for everyone.

The family somehow managed to avoid a major emotional outburst for about ten weeks, during which Sharon endured her chemotherapy treatments. Then the girls' report cards came home. Ron told the girls they weren't applying themselves, and they both ran off to their rooms crying. Sharon told Ron to ease up on them and reminded him that everyone was stressed out. He said nothing and left the house.

At her next appointment, Sharon told her oncologist how hopeless she was feeling. The doctor prescribed an antidepressant and referred her to a psychiatrist for further evaluation. By the time Sharon had her appointment with the psychiatrist, she couldn't sleep at night and was unable to work. The psychiatrist decided to admit her to a local hospital.

After two and a half weeks in the hospital her depression lifted enough that she could go home. Her girls were excited to see her and Ron was civil. Two days later, however, Ron told Sharon he was leaving and wanted a divorce. Sharon withdrew to her bed for the rest of the day. Over the next few months, she did little more than eat and sleep and keep her doctors' appointments. Each chemotherapy session left her nauseated for several days. Her daughters made their own meals, did their homework, and got themselves off to school without her help. Hardly anyone spoke with each other.

After four months, the chemotherapy sessions were tapered down and Sharon's physical health began to improve. At her six-month checkup, she was told she was cancer free. The diagnosis didn't sink in for several days, but when it did, Sharon awoke with a smile that matched the sunshine of the morning. She fixed breakfast for her daughters, who were surprised to find their mother up and smiling. They left for school with lighter hearts, too. Sharon was able to read a novel for the first time since her cancer diagnosis.

Her cancer treatment progressed to radiation therapy every three weeks for six more treatments, but the physical effects were much less debilitating than those associated with the chemotherapy. She started back to work on a limited basis and realized just how easily she became tired. However, working helped her feel normal again and gave her a new sense of hope that maybe her ordeal was coming to an end.

A year after her cancer diagnosis, Sharon was back to work full time, her girls were happy again in school most of the time, her divorce was proceeding through the negotiation process, and her body was beginning to feel whole again. She cried herself to sleep sometimes and periodically railed at God, but on the whole she felt blessed to be alive and healthy again and to have her daughters to love and to live for.

I met Sharon four years after her diagnosis of cancer. She was happy, her daughters had blossomed into beautiful young women, her relationship with her ex-husband rankled at times but she mostly kept her sense of humor, and her work filled her with satisfaction. She found a peacefulness in her soul as she accepted that God had given her the strength to survive a series of ordeals that she never expected.

She summed up her experiences in a brief conversation with me by saying, "I have learned how easily I forget the many blessings in my life and how easily I become preoccupied with the small and mundane irritations of life. Now what means most to me is to be able to wake up every morning, kiss my kids, say hello to the sun or the clouds, watch the birds fly, and realize that life is a gift and that I have been blessed to know its worst and its best."

I said a silent amen.

SUGGESTIONS FOR CHANGE. You've just about finished this book. Take a break to celebrate. You've earned it!

Epilogue

My Wish for Your Journey in Pursuit of Happiness, Love, and Understanding

Be tenacious in your journey to family healing. Never give up. If you meet a roadblock, find a detour. Redefine the path to your goal or reframe the goal itself. Temporarily retreat to thoughtfulness and creativity and to a place where you can rekindle your connection to meaning and joy. Allow yourself to know when you're discouraged without giving in to discouragement. It takes time for the good work you do to soak in around you. Keep at it. Believe in it. Once you have planted the seeds of change, give them time to grow.

Parenting is an enormous subject, so you probably still have questions. Appendix D provides a list for further reading. Professional and other organizations are listed in appendix C. Your questions to the author, comments about the book, and personal stories are welcome. Contact me through my Web site at www.FamilyHealing.com.

May your family journey bring you lasting joy and satisfaction.

Appendix A

COMMENTS ON THE PARENTING QUESTIONNAIRE

Here are my answers *in italics* to the parenting questionnaire on pages 9, 10, and 11:

1. I want to be a good parent.

   I hope this is true.

2. I love my children no matter how badly they misbehave.

   I hope this is true, too. It is vitally important to separate our love for our children from how they behave, to be able to say, "I love you, and you are going to your room now for hitting your sister, and I love you."

3. I feel out of control with my children too much of the time.

   Any time we feel out of control with our children is a time to be concerned. We can acquire many skills to help us stay in bounds.

4. My parents gave me good models for how to be a good parent.

   I hope this is true. Most of us get some good guidance from our parents. What is missing we have to learn in other ways.

5. My ideas for dealing with trouble usually help make the situation better.

   The more ideas you have, the better. The more real choices we have in the face of trouble, the more likely we will have a good choice.

6. I can enjoy rebellious children.

   I hope you said yes. If not, you probably have ghosts to visit. Rebelliousness is a sign of character and confidence. It can also be a sign of desperation. We do better to foster constructive rebellion, where we help the rebel to find satisfaction in his own way of doing things, rather than accepting a power struggle where one of us must lose.

7. I can be firm with my children when I need to be.

    Loving parents hold the line when they need to. We don't do our children any favors by letting them get away with misbehaving. They learn responsibility through facing proportionate, loving consequences for their successes and failures. It is better to learn about consequences within the confines of a loving relationship at home than to discover the harshness of consequences out in a world that bears no love for them.

8. I can redirect my children from their misbehavior most of the time.

    Especially with small children, redirection into constructive play earns a double benefit. We get them to do what we find acceptable, and their behavior is reinforced by the fun that follows.

9. I can get my family to solve problems together.

    This is an important skill to develop if you aren't already proficient. The key is good listening. People get irritable and uncooperative when they feel unheard and unappreciated or are mentally ill. Once you learn what is really bothering someone, you have a chance to help make the situation better.

10. My natural tendency is to give my child a second chance.

    Generosity is a virtue in child rearing as long as it is accompanied with firm and loving discipline. Third and fourth chances for one offense begin to reinforce irresponsibility. Set standards you know your children can meet, then hold them accountable. This way they learn social skills, self-discipline, and respect for others' needs and wishes.

11. My children can make me laugh.

    Teaching our children appropriate use of humor is teaching them how to get along in the world. Loving humor can heal most wounds. Reinforce humor that is honest and inclusive anytime you can. Ultimately we will hold our children to standards of love, honesty, and respect. We model these values when we honor humor that says, "You caught me and I love you."

12. Sometimes I dread being with one or more of my children.

    Sometimes one of our children is more difficult to love and that child will often become a special concern. Special children require special strategies for parenting. Before pinning on yourself the label of "bad parent," seek help for the specific problems you are having. We are not born knowing how to parent each of our different children well.

13. I have physically or mentally injured one of my children.

    This is difficult to admit and yet very important. It is very hard to stay in bounds all the time. When we say something harsh or react physically against our children, we are responsible, no matter what the provocation. Each of us is always responsible for what we do. If we have erred, we should make amends and work to resolve the concurrent stresses that led us to misbehave. We should hold our children to this same standard, too.

14. I can predict when trouble is likely to erupt in my family.

    This ability is very helpful. Awareness of the emotional realities within the family gives us opportunities to plan ahead. It is more effective to find ways to defuse and heal emotional pain than to clean up after eruptions. Learning the patterns of conflict opens new possibilities for creative problem solving.

15. My partner and I work well together in raising our children.

    Partnership is best. Working out a partnership takes intentional focus and communication, a sense of humor, and willingness to back each other up within the parameters of loving discipline.

16. There are alcoholics in my family.

    Alcoholism in families can be devastating for children. When we grow up with an alcoholic parent, we learn to accommodate the uncertainties of brief and prolonged emotional absences, blunted feelings, secrets, denial, fear, loss, and maybe emotional or physical violence. This then becomes the norm for creating our own families, and we tend to introduce our children to similar injuries.

17. Serious depression or anxiety problems run in my family.

    Learn to recognize the signs, so when mental disorders emerge within your own family, you get appropriate help early, rather than suffering the painful consequences of an untreated disorder.

18. I had some very rough times with my own parents.

    These times are likely sources of ghost intrusions into your parenting responses now. Be especially careful when dealing with your children concerning issues where you had bad experiences growing up so you don't simply recreate in your family the chaos and pain that you endured as a child.

19. Someone in my own family was sexually or physically abused.

    You need professional help. The more love and support we get for ourselves and for anyone else who was injured, the more likely we are to heal. Abusers are invariably themselves survivors of abuse or a mental disorder or both and may be so caught up in their own lies and denials that they cannot cooperate in the healing. If so, they must leave the home. The challenge of abuse in families is to hold all members accountable for their own needs, feelings, and actions. Full acceptance of responsibility for abusiveness, followed by appropriate amends, lays a foundation for healing and possibly forgiveness. Honesty and love are the balm that can speed healing.

20. I would seek professional help if I thought my family needed it.

    Reluctance to expose a family's "dirty laundry" to a stranger is both natural and understandable. But don't let it stop you if your family needs outside help. Talk with somebody. Ask others about professional help they have received. A good referral can make a world of difference with complex disorders and family problems.

21. My parents encourage my efforts to be a good parent.

    Even from a distance, loving, understanding parents are a blessing. Give them a chance to listen, at least, and tell you they love you. Figure out what you need. Then, if they cannot provide it, find someone who can. In a pinch, imagine what they would provide if they were emotionally able. You might be amazed at how much better you feel.

22. I have a supportive extended family available to help me.

    A supportive family acts as a buffer against isolation and is a place to turn for help and resources. If you don't have a supportive family, then you need to find support and resources elsewhere. These are available in varying quantity and quality in many communities but require a search. The information in the appendices may help you get started.

23. I have supportive friends who sometimes join in my family activities.

    Again, friends are a buffer against isolation and helplessness. Let them know what's going on with you and in your family. Most likely they will not be able to solve your problems, but their listening will empower you to think of new ideas and new resources.

24. I have meaningful friends and activities of my own, separate from my family.

The more we lead lives that allow us full expression of our personal interests and talents, the better model we create for our children to do the same. Happiness comes with doing the activities that nourish our curiosity, creativity, and friendships.

25. I belong to a community of people where I feel safe and accepted.

Finding a community for your family is an important task of good parenting. Healthy families usually are connected to multiple communities formed around shared neighborhood, activities, interests, and religion. The rewards are profound when we find safe and accepting communities.

26. My family belongs to a community of faith or mutual support.

Faith communities have many ways to support troubled families. So do some community groups organized for common childcare, economic empowerment, and neighborhood improvement. The key is finding people genuinely interested in helping each other.

27. I notice beauty when I encounter it.

Nature provides an always-ready battery charger for our souls. Beauty brings us peace, energy, and rededication to life. Soak it up. Beauty is everywhere—in flowers, storm clouds, smiles, kind deeds, and starry nights. And it's free.

28. I find life miraculous at times.

This speaks of our ability to appreciate and celebrate the wonderful intricacies that abound in life. Start by admiring a newborn baby and let the feeling grow as you look more closely at every marvelous living thing.

29. I can raise healthy children.

Yes. You can!

30. I believe I am a good parent.

This belief comes from seeing your children thrive under your care. If you are loving and honest and consistently encourage cooperation, you should raise happy, secure, and responsible children. If you don't, either you are blind to something you are doing that is undermining your efforts, or your children have special needs you have yet to recognize.

By now you have a more conscious awareness of your parenting strengths and weaknesses. Make a commitment today to build on your strengths and to improve your weaker skills.

Appendix B

COMMON MENTAL DISORDERS

Descriptions of nine major categories of mental disorders are presented below.[30] If you think you fit the description for any of these disorders, you still may or may not have the disorder. An evaluation with a physician, psychiatrist, clinical psychologist, or in some cases a registered nurse practitioner is required to make a diagnosis. Most of these disorders are very treatable with some combination of medicine and/or psychotherapy. If anyone in your family is experiencing significant difficulty in his or her health, school, work, or personal life because of these symptoms, then that person would benefit greatly from a professional evaluation, and so would the rest of the family.

The terms "mental disorder" and "mental illness" are generally synonymous and I use them interchangeably. Formally, a *disorder* meets explicit diagnostic criteria and requires a rating of the severity of symptoms, so it is a more specific and technical term. An *illness* refers more to the obvious disability a person shows. I have used the term *disorder* in the text in hopes that it feels less stigmatizing.

Depression

Clinical depression is a disabling medical disorder characterized by both physical and cognitive (mental) symptoms. Depression clearly is passed along in the genes in some families. It is a physical disorder of the brain and has a number of measurable physical consequences. Brain scans, for example, show that parts of the brain are much less active during depression than when the same person is not depressed. Severe depression may even cause (or be caused by) shrinkage of neuronal dendrites in the brain, the branch-like interconnections between brain cells that allow them to communicate with each other. So depression is not someone choosing to be lazy. Rather, the loss of energy, loss of interest in usually pleasurable activity, and loss of motivation are likely the consequences of depressed brain function.

Dan described his moderate level of depression this way:

> Looking back I realize I was having a much harder time getting out of bed in the morning for more than a week. And that was after a restless night's sleep. I kept waking up and then had a hard time getting back to sleep. During the day it feels like someone pulled the plug on my energy and made me wear a lead jacket. I've lost interest in just about everything except video games. Even my girlfriend can't motivate me to do things with her. A friend tried to make me laugh and I just snapped at him. I mean I was rude. I feel horrible. I drag myself to school every day and then I can't stay focused in class. I fall asleep or my mind numbs out. I catch myself thinking how nice it would be if I went to sleep and didn't wake up.

If Dan's depression were to become more severe, he might be unable to get out of bed or get himself to school because of his low energy and loss of motivation. His fleeting thoughts about dying might seem like sensible ideas to escape the awful feelings. Depression is a nasty, sometimes lethal disorder. To use Dan's word, it can make you feel horrible.

Depression was the most common medical diagnosis in several studies of prepaid primary healthcare clinics. Different people experience different combinations of depressive symptoms. To be diagnosed with depression a person needs to experience five or more major symptoms over a period of one or more weeks. In a 1992 study of adults nearly 20 percent of the U.S. population met diagnostic criteria for clinical depression at some time in their lives. These people reported enough low energy, loss of interest, and low mood to interfere with their work, health, or personal life. Depression can be mildly to severely disabling. People who are depressed are more likely to kill themselves than people who are not depressed.

The good news is that depression in nearly all its forms is very treatable with a combination of antidepressant medications, appropriate activities and exercise, and psychotherapy as needed. The goal of treatment for depression should always be 100 percent remission.

To find help, start with your family doctor. If you know someone who received good help with his or her depression, ask for a referral, or tell your local crisis line volunteer that you are looking for treatment for possible depression. Don't allow an active depressive disorder in your family to go untreated.

Anxiety and Panic Disorders

Anxiety is a common, normal response to possible danger. We all can get queasy looking over the edge of a balcony or a bridge, and most of us get butterflies when we first speak in front of an audience. Anxiety *disorders* are marked by *excessive* anxiety—clearly out of proportion to the danger—that interferes with our ability to perform and to regain a comfortable composure.

This is how Katie explained her anxiety:

> I'm nearly always a little nervous around other people, especially
> when I'm away from home. If someone I don't know walks up to me,
> my heart starts pounding and I feel edgy. My hands get shaky and my
> voice cracks sometimes. When I feel like this, I just want to be at home.
> It gets worse when I'm stuck in a crowd or I get too far from home. If
> I think I'm going to faint or throw up, then it really gets bad. I don't
> think I've ever had a panic attack, but I've heard about them and what
> I feel seems pretty close some of the time.

People with anxiety disorders become easily frightened and have difficulty calming down. In the study of the U.S. population mentioned above, nearly 10 percent of the adult population could be diagnosed with an anxiety disorder. That means anxiety severe enough to interfere with a person's health, work, or family relationships. Fear in situations of real danger is both healthy and protective. Excessive anxiety limits a person's ability to think clearly or to tolerate situations that arouse anxiety. Normal activities may become severely restricted as a person avoids more and more situations that stir up unbearable anxiety.

Panic attacks are the most acute form of anxiety and the most terrifying. Women are somewhat more likely than men to suffer from panic anxiety.

Karen described a panic attack like this:

> I was driving down the freeway when all of a sudden I got scared. My head started to feel full and then I started to feel dizzy. My heart was pounding so hard I thought I might be having a heart attack. My hands got so sweaty they felt slippery on the steering wheel. I felt lucky that I was able to pull over without an accident. Thankfully I knew what it was because I had something like this happen a year ago. Otherwise I would have thought I was going to die. Even then it took me nearly twenty minutes to calm down before I could drive home.

Those experiencing their first panic attack and people with severe panic sometimes go to the emergency room out of fear they are having a heart attack. However, unless you have significant heart disease, a panic attack is no more dangerous to your body than running as hard as you can for a quarter mile.

Anxiety disorders are probably passed along in the genes in some families and are sometimes evident in early childhood. Severe or chronic anxiety can be severely limiting and warrants a psychiatric evaluation. Current medications and psychotherapy are very effective against most forms of anxiety. Recovery is the norm. Cognitive behavioral therapy is particularly effective with anxiety problems and probably more effective over the long run than medication alone.

Depression and anxiety together are an especially painful and disabling combination and are associated with higher suicide risk than either one alone. Don't allow a persistent anxiety disorder in your family to go untreated.

Bipolar Disorder (Formerly Manic-Depressive Illness)

Bipolar disorders are disorders of mood and thought patterns characterized by disruptive cycling of moods between depression and hypomania or mania. Hypomania ("low" mania, or manic symptoms without psychosis) typically leads to days or weeks of poor sleep (less than five hours a night), racing thoughts, impulsive behavior (overspending, working on many new projects), excessive sociability, heightened sexual interest, grandiose ideas about one's self and work, and either euphoric good feelings or marked irritability. Hypomanic mood swings are now diagnosed as a Bipolar II Disorder if periods of both clinical depression and hypomania occur.

Patrick described his hypomanic disorder this way:

> I was about eighteen when I first got really sick. I'd been depressed on and off through junior high school, but I didn't think much about it until I got hypomanic my junior year in high school. My friends thought I was high on something. I'd tried pot and a little speed with them. But the speed made me feel really crazy so I stopped doing any of that stuff. I started feeling really happy. I'd stay up half the night or all night and play music or compose new songs. One time I wrote the world's greatest short story, which didn't make much sense when I read it months later. I was hitting on all the girls and some of the guys (that only got me punched out once) and talking to anybody who'd listen. They kicked me out of class for talking too much or just not paying attention. I couldn't sit still for more than ten seconds. I never have heard voices or thought I was God or anything, but I've been pretty high with no drugs in my system.

Bipolar mood swings often run in families and seem to segregate into two distinct disorders, one with and one without psychotic highs.

Mania is the hallmark of a Bipolar I Disorder and is defined by Bipolar II symptoms plus psychotic symptoms. Hallucinations and delusions characterize manic psychosis—hearing voices, seeing things that are not there, having ideas of reference (believing the television or radio or other public media are speaking directly to you), reading special messages into everyday events, believing you are someone you are not.

Dr. Kay Redfield Jamison was a clinical psychologist on the psychiatry faculty at UCLA when she had her first manic episode. She describes in a powerful and unnerving book titled *An Unquiet Mind* how as her illness progressed she became consumed by delusions of grandeur and hallucinations (see appendix D). Of particular note is her description of her own initial refusal to accept treatment and how much she liked the extra energy and ability to think creatively. Someone experiencing manic mood swings frequently loves the experience but loses the ability to see his or her problems accurately and loses the judgment needed to avoid costly behaviors like spending money way beyond one's means or having an affair. People who are manic are also much less likely to seek help because they feel so good and don't believe they need help.

Both forms of bipolar disorder can be very disabling, depending on how impulsive and out of touch with reality a person becomes and how well people around them know what is helpful. Clearly, psychosis is reason to seek immediate psychiatric help, but so also is significant hypomania or depression. A competent evaluation of bipolar symptoms will save you a world of grief over time. Hypomanic impulsiveness occasionally leads a person into bankruptcy from overspending followed by disabling depression.

These major mood swing disorders affect between 1 and 2 percent of the general population and can occur in young children (see *The Bipolar Child* in appendix D).

Posttraumatic Stress Disorder (PTSD)

Overwhelming trauma creates intrusive anxieties that can become severely disabling. Nightmares are common in which the trauma is played over and over, often disrupting sleep. Daytime flashbacks usually point to posttraumatic stress disorder (PTSD)—a person is suddenly reliving the traumatic event as if it were happening again right now in a full-blown sensory replay including terror and smells.

Paul survived eight months of active combat in Vietnam in 1969 and still has nightmares and flashbacks of his buddy dying right next to him from a chest wound. Harriet's older brother raped her repeatedly over several years and threatened to kill her if she told anyone. Twenty years later when her daughter reached the age when the trauma started, Harriet began to have nightmares and intrusive flashbacks.

The earlier in life a severely traumatizing event occurs, the more likely a person will develop PTSD. Soldiers who were abused as children are more likely to develop war-related PTSD than their nonabused comrades. In addition, the earlier and the more overwhelming the abuse, the more severe the later anxiety and the more intrusive the memories.

Simple PTSD from a single trauma is usually quite treatable with psychotherapy that helps to desensitize the person to the horror of the overwhelming event. Antianxiety medication can relieve overwhelming discomfort during the early stages of desensitization therapy. Complex PTSD, as develops for some veterans of prolonged and horrific warfare and for many survivors of severe childhood abuse, is much more difficult to treat effectively. The strategies are similar, but the treatment demands great patience in the desensitization process and may require heavy doses of tranquilizing medications. Recovery from severe PTSD definitely requires the help of well-trained professionals. Self-help guides for working with less severe PTSD are available (see appendix D).

Substance Abuse Disorders

Alcohol is the most commonly abused substance in the United States, followed by marijuana. Cocaine, methamphetamines (speed), hallucinogens, and heroin also take a heavy toll on the health of many people. Often the abuser is self-medicating an underlying anxiety disorder, depression, or posttraumatic stress disorder. Alcoholism runs in some families and in some ethnic groups where essential breakdown enzymes for alcohol are missing. Clearly, some people are more susceptible to the effects of alcohol than others and are more likely to become addicted.

I read recently that thirteen million Americans are admitted alcoholics! And Alcoholics Anonymous is widely regarded as the single most effective self-help organization anywhere. Early-stage alcoholism is characterized by use of escalating amounts of alcohol on a near daily basis with increasing preoccupation with new opportunities to drink and denial of problems related to this pattern of drinking. A person with middle-stage alcoholism organizes his or her whole life around consuming alcohol and hiding its effects. Blackouts may be frequent and the need for next-morning sedation is common. Late-stage alcoholism is marked by obsessive consumption of alcohol, serious health effects including recurrent blackouts, lost marriages and families, lost jobs, and lost self-esteem. Disability can be total, the person may become homeless, and the disorder can be fatal.

Treatment requires enforced sobriety and appropriate treatment of underlying medical (including mental) disorders. Individual and family therapy is sometimes very helpful if the parties are willing participants. Statistically, the best outcomes for alcohol treatment include attending AA meetings regularly and taking Antabuse (its generic name is disulfiram, a benign medicine except in the presence of alcohol, when it makes a person vomit).

Like alcoholism, marijuana abuse can be difficult to treat because a person may be reluctant to acknowledge that it's a problem. Again, when disability occurs in one's health, occupation, or close relationships, a disorder can be diagnosed and treatment should be pursued.

Most health insurance companies have special contracts with treatment programs for alcohol and other drug abuse and are a good source of information about available programs.

Attention Deficit Disorder with or without Hyperactivity

Attention deficit disorders with or without hyperactivity (ADHD/ADD) are childhood disorders that affect between 3 and 5 percent of America's school-age children, depending on how severe the qualifying symptoms are. ADD and ADHD can create major disability for children and deserve careful evaluation. We're not talking about snuffing out high energy and spontaneity. We're talking about helping children whose ability to screen out noise is so faulty that as hard as they try, they cannot stay focused enough to keep up with their peers in school or at play. They typically fall farther and farther behind as they pass through school, or they become the class scapegoat, clown, delinquent, or dropout. Distractible kids without hyperactivity often escape detection and suffer from lower grades and less social success than nondistractible children of comparable age and ability.

ADD reminds me of a radio without a noise filter. There is so much static and interference from other signals that you can't hear the station you're trying to tune in. Like taking your noisy radio into a quiet room so you can listen better, people with milder forms of ADD and ADHD respond well to changes in their environment that provide fewer distractions and more structure. To help these children, quiet their surroundings and make direct eye contact with them when you want their attention. Not uncommonly, children who have attention deficit disorder can cope at home but find the many distractions of a classroom too much to handle. They need immediate feedback to keep their attention, like video games and action cartoons. The more distractible they are, the more likely they are to have trouble keeping friends or playing group games or team sports.

Successful treatment for these children requires special accommodations at home and school. When environmental modifications aren't enough, appropriate levels of a stimulant medication often prove helpful. Stimulant medications turn the noise filters on so ADD children have a chance to focus on the station that's most important, such as their parent or teacher or book or homework assignment.

Concern about fostering drug dependence in children must be balanced against the low self-esteem and poor academic and social progress that often accompany ADD and ADHD. Studies of adolescent drug abuse have shown that youth with untreated ADHD are actually more likely to abuse drugs and that appropriate treatment of ADD and ADHD can protect youngsters from misguided attempts at self-medication.

Schizophrenia and Other Psychoses

Schizophrenic disorders are characterized by the more or less continuous presence of positive symptoms, such as hallucinations, delusions, and distorted thought processes, or negative symptoms, such as flattened emotions, sparseness of speech, and "wooden" facial and body movements. Often both positive and negative symptoms are present. Unlike the cycling of symptoms in a bipolar disorder, symptoms of schizophrenic disorders seldom go away completely. A person with schizophrenia often speaks without the usual emotional modulations of healthy speech, has a limited range of emotions he or she can share, has difficulty with strong feelings and close relationships, and has unusual thought patterns, sometimes including nonsense talk or not talking at all. These psychoses are severely disabling chronic disorders that require psychiatric help.

Psychotic symptoms can occur for reasons other than schizophrenia. Severely depressed or medically ill patients will sometimes hallucinate. Psychosis may also occur as a severe side effect of some medications. Depending on the reason for the psychotic symptoms, the psychosis may be short-lived or chronic. Hallucinations that occur as you are just falling asleep or just waking up are usually normal phenomena. Most psychotic experiences leave lasting fears of further psychosis. I recommend that any psychotic episode be thoroughly evaluated by a psychiatrist, even if it is drug induced.

Autism

Children with autistic traits seem odd and socially awkward. They tend to avoid direct eye contact, and their facial expressions seem unresponsive to the social cues around them. (If they smile, for example, it will commonly be in response to something in their own thoughts rather than in response to another person.) Their gestures may be stiff and behaviors tend toward repetitive or stereotyped activities, like flapping their hands, talking endlessly on one subject, or playing the same game over and over again. Intense preoccupation with a limited range of interests may keep them from bonding with other children.

Autistic children require professional evaluation and an appropriate array of treatments that are designed for the individual child. Occasionally medication can be helpful, but more often these children need specially structured environments that support them in their strengths, which can be considerable, and help them compensate for their limitations. Higher functioning children with autism can be trained to approximate more normal social interaction, which can greatly decrease their overall disability.

Bulimia, Anorexia, and Obesity

Bulimia nervosa and anorexia nervosa are disorders of mainly young women and a few young men who develop distorted perceptions of body weight and shape and as a consequence become obsessed with eating and weight control. Obesity affects a wide range of men and women, has both medical and psychological roots, and may also be associated with distortions of body image.

Bulimia is defined by binge eating followed in a short time by inappropriate ways of losing weight, typically vomiting or purging with laxatives. Leslie described her bulimia this way:

> I think about eating all the time, especially when I'm stressed about something. I usually get up in the middle of the night so no one sees me and stuff myself on ice cream or cookies or whatever I can find. It's like I have to do it even though it's totally embarrassing when someone catches me. Then I go and throw up in the toilet and go back to bed. I started doing it back in junior high and I can't seem to stop myself.

The last decade has seen an epidemic of bulimia among college-age women. Members of one sorority told me about times they lined up for the bathroom to purge in the middle of the night.

Anorexia is an illness involving body perception characterized by a potentially life-threatening fear of gaining weight. A person with a more severe form of anorexia develops a delusional belief that she or he is obese along with a morbid fear of gaining weight, when in fact she or he is dangerously underweight. Young people with anorexia see themselves as fat even when they may look to others like famine victims. Weight loss can become severe, requiring hospitalization and even intravenous feeding to save the person's life. Recent use of certain antidepressant medications has sometimes proved helpful.

Mood disorders, excessive anxiety, and substance abuse are commonly associated problems in people with bulimia or anorexia, sometimes predating the onset of the eating disorder. These can be highly stressful illnesses for families as well as the affected individual and definitely warrant appropriate evaluation. (See appendix D for further reading.)

Obesity is a growing problem in the United States as Americans seem to eat higher calorie foods and exercise less. Easy accumulation of excess body fat clearly runs in some families and has a number of physical causes that warrant medical evaluation. Among people with psychological reasons for becoming seriously overweight, the most common in my practice have been women who were sexually abused as children and who now maintain a disfiguring weight in the delusional belief that they will thereby be safe from further assault. These women have often failed commercial weight loss programs because of their panic at appearing sexually attractive again. For sexual abuse survivors whose obesity creates serious medical risks, weight loss may require intensive psychotherapy as well as nutritional help with a diet plan. Medication for associated depression and anxiety may also help. Overeaters Anonymous is helpful for some.

Appendix C

MENTAL HEALTH RESOURCES

The following organizations can give you additional information about mental health problems and guide you toward professional help. For updated referrals, visit my Web site at www.FamilyHealing.com/organizations.

American Academy of Child and
   Adolescent Psychiatry
3615 Wisconsin Avenue N.W.
Washington, DC 20016-3007
800-333-7636, 202-966-7300
www.aacap.org

American Psychiatric Association
1400 K Street N.W.
Washington, DC 20005
888-35PSYCH (888-357-7924)
www.psych.org

Anxiety Disorders Association
   of America
11900 Parklawn Drive, Suite 100
Rockville, MD 20852
301-231-9350
www.adaa.org

National Alliance for the Mentally Ill
Colonial Place Three
2107 Wilson Boulevard, Suite 300
Arlington, VA 22201-3042
800-950-NAMI (6264)
www.nami.org

National Depressive and Manic-
   Depressive Association
730 N. Frankin Street, Suite 501
Chicago, IL 60610-7204
800-826-3632, 312-642-0049
www.ndmda.org

National Foundation for
   Depressive Illness, Inc.
P.O. Box 2257
New York, NY 10116
800-239-1265
www.depression.org

National Institute of Mental Health
NIMH Public Inquiries
6001 Executive Boulevard,
Room 8184, MSC 9663
Bethesda, MD 20892-9663
301-443-4513
www.nimh.nih.gov

National Mental Health Association
1021 Prince Street
Alexandria, VA 22314-2971
703-684-7722
www.nmha.org

Obsessive-Compulsive Foundation,
   Inc.
337 Notch Hill Road
North Branford, CT 06471
203-315-2190
www.ocfoundation.org

*Other organizations referred to
in the text:*

Mothers Against Violence in
   America (MAVIA)
105 14th Avenue, Suite 2-A
Seattle, WA 98122
206-323-2303, 800-897-7697
www.mavia.org

Mothers Against Drunk Driving
   (MADD)
P.O. Box 541688
Dallas, TX 75354-1688
800-GET-MADD
www.madd.org

Mothers for Police Accountability
P.O. Box 22886
Seattle, WA 98122
206-329-2033

Appendix D

RECOMMENDED READINGS: A SELECT BIBLIOGRAPHY

Child and Adolescent Development

American Academy of Child and Adolescent Psychiatry. *Your Child: Emotional, Behavioral and Cognitive Development from Infancy to Preadolescence: What's Normal, What's Not, and When to Seek Help.* Edited by David Pruitt. New York: HarperCollins Publishers, 1998.

American Academy of Child and Adolescent Psychiatry. *Your Adolescent: Emotional, Behavioral and Cognitive Development from Early Adolescence through the Teen Years: What's Normal, What's Not, and When to Seek Help.* Edited by David Pruitt. New York: HarperCollins Publishers, 1999.

These are two state-of-the-art books on normal child and adolescent development, common problems, and ways to solve them.

Brazelton, T. Berry, M.D. *Touchpoints: Your Child's Emotional and Behavioral Development.* Reading, Mass.: A Merloyd Lawrence Book, Perseus Books, 1992.

Heir to Dr. Spock, Dr. Brazelton offers a world of experience and gentle, knowing calm to anxious parents—what to expect and what to do from pregnancy through six years.

Davis, Laura and Janis Keyser. *Becoming the Parent You Want to Be: A Sourcebook of Strategies for the First Five Years.* New York: Broadway Books, 1997.

An up-to-date, empowering, easy-to-use guide that helps build a parent's confidence. The stories of other parents make it a rich source of ideas and affirmation.

Fraiberg, Selma. *The Magic Years.* New York: Charles Scribner's Sons, 1959.

This classic description of early childhood helps us remember how beautiful, fragile, and smart our children are.

Ilg, Frances L., M.D., Louise B. Ames, Ph.D., and Sydney M. Baker, M.D. *Child Behavior: The Classic Childcare Manual from the Gesell Institute of Human Development.* New York: Perennial, 1992.

My wife and I raised our children on the early edition of this book. It helps you recognize disorganization in your child's behavior that foretells the next surge of developmental progress.

Karr-Morse, Robin, and Meredith Wiley. *Ghosts from the Nursery: Tracing the Roots of Violence.* New York: The Atlantic Monthly Press, 1997.

Toxic chemicals and abusive emotions in utero and through the first three years of life can permanently impair a child's ability to bond with others, leading to lives burdened with disability and disinhibited aggression.

Orenstein, Peggy. *Schoolgirls: Young Women, Self-Esteem, and the Confidence Gap.* New York: Anchor Books, Random House, 1994.

A disturbing account of how and why young women suffer low self-esteem in our culture. Orenstein starts with a national survey commissioned by the American Association of University Women in 1992 and follows girls from two very different middle schools for a whole school year.

Vernon, Ann, Ph.D., and Rahdi Al-Mabuk, Ph.D. *What Growing Up Is All About: A Parent's Guide to Child and Adolescent Development.* Champaign, Ill.: Research Press, 1995.

A concise, well-written summary of children's developmental stages and the parenting styles that help or hinder you or make it harder with each stage.

Adult Development—Finding Ourselves

Hanh, Thich Nhat. *Being Peace*. Berkeley: Parallax Press, 1987.

"If we are peaceful, if we are happy, we can blossom like a flower, and everyone in our family, our entire society, will benefit from our peace."

Peck, M. Scott, M.D. *The Road Less Traveled: A New Psychology of Love, Traditional Values and Spiritual Growth*. New York: Simon and Schuster, 1978.

Still one of my favorite books on the search for love and meaning in our lives.

Marital, Family, and Stepfamily Issues—More Help

Einstein, Elizabeth. *The Stepfamily: Living, Loving and Learning*. Boston: Shambhala Publications, 1982.

This book won the National Media Award from the American Psychological Association. May be out of print. Try your local library.

Hendrix, Harville, Ph.D., and Helen Hendrix, M.A., M.L.A. *Giving the Love that Heals: A Guide for Parents*. New York: Pocket Books, Simon and Schuster, 1997.

Hendrix, Harville, Ph.D. *Getting the Love You Want: A Guide for Couples*. New York: Pocket Books, Simon and Schuster, 1990.

Both of these books bring a huge heart and wise counsel to struggling parents and couples.

McKay, Matthew, Ph.D., Patrick Fanning, and Kim Paleg, Ph.D. *Couple Skills: Making Your Relationship Work*. Oakland: New Harbinger Publications, Inc., 1994.

I continue to be impressed with the books from New Harbinger Publications (800-748-6273) and its founder, Matthew McKay. This is a practical, skill-building book for couples.

Rubin, Jeffrey, Ph.D., and Carol Rubin, M.D. *When Families Fight: How to Handle Conflict with Those You Love.* New York: Ballantine Books, Random House, 1989.

Yet another excellent book to spring from Harvard Negotiation Project alumni. This book reads almost like a novel yet is full of wisdom, common sense, and love.

Parenting—Ideas, References

See also appendix G, Parent Skills Training.

Blechman, Elaine A., Ph.D. *Solving Child Behavior Problems at Home and at School.* Champaign, Ill.: Research Press, 1985.

(See comments in appendix G, page 281.)

Clarke, Jean Illsley. *Self-Esteem: A Family Affair.* San Francisco: Harper-SanFrancisco, 1978.

Another classic. "A buffet table of options" for struggling parents or parents who simply want to improve their ability to raise confident, caring children.

Drew, Naomi. *Peaceful Parents, Peaceful Kids: Practical Ways to Create a Calm and Happy Home.* New York: Kensington Publishing Corp., 2000.

Seventeen keys to peaceful parenting start with "#1 Peace begins with me, #2 I have made my home a place of kind words, and #3 I catch my children in the act of positive behaviors and praise them immediately, specifically, and sincerely." It keeps getting better.

Frankel, Fred, Ph.D. *Good Friends Are Hard to Find: Help Your Child Find, Make and Keep Friends.* Los Angeles: Perspective Publishing, 1996.

This friendly, attractive book is a must for families with socially unhappy children. Special chapters help you and your child to deal with teasing, bullying, rumors, and more.

Glenn, Stephen H., Ph.D., and Jane Nelsen, Ed.D. *Raising Self-Reliant Children in a Self-Indulgent World: Seven Building Blocks for Developing Capable Young People.* Rev. ed. Roseville, Calif.: Prima Publishing, 2000.

Joslin, Karen Renshaw. *Positive Parenting from A to Z.* New York: Ballantine Books, 1994.

Positive encouragement and practical tips for a wide range of child-rearing topics arranged as a reference guide. A loving, effective mom sharing her wisdom.

Patterson, Gerald R. *Families: Applications of Social Learning to Family Life.* Rev. ed. Champaign, Ill.: Research Press, 1975.

Still my first choice for basic skill building for parents. Chapters on Social Reinforcers, Accidental Training, Behavior Management Skills, Behavior Change Techniques, and help with specific problems such as tantrums, bed-wetting, lying, and aggression.

Pipher, Mary, Ph.D. *The Shelter of Each Other: Rebuilding Our Families.* New York: Ballantine Books, Random House, 1996.

A compelling call to recognize the siren song of cultural consumerism. Instead seek time together with family and therapy based on love, resilience, and community with your neighbors.

Riley, Douglas A., Ph.D. *The Defiant Child: A Parent's Guide to Oppositional Defiant Disorder.* Dallas: Taylor Publishing, 1997.

Supportive professional advice for putting you back in charge of your insistently unruly child. Helps you develop a firm, steady, loving way to dis-cipline.

Scott, Virginia, George Doub, and Peggy Runnels. *Raising a Loving Family.* Holbrook, Mass.: Adams Media Corporation, 1999.

Developed from the Family Wellness seminars, this book presents the seven characteristics of healthy families and how you can build them into your family.

Sloane, Howard N. *The Good Kid Book: How to Solve the 16 Most Common Behavior Problems.* Champaign, Ill.: Research Press, 1979.

This book has the details, star charts, and friendly illustrations for parents who can't seem to make the usual behavior modification programs work. Don't forget good humor and consistency!

Negotiating—Crucial Skills for Healthy Families

Ury, William, Ph.D. *Getting Past No: Negotiating Your Way from Confrontation to Cooperation.* Rev. ed. New York: Bantam Books, 1993.

This is one of the best books you will find anywhere on how to get along, full of practical ideas and loving realism. Based on ideas developed with Roger Fisher in the Harvard Negotiation Project.

Ury, William, Ph.D. *The Third Side: Why We Fight and How We Can Stop.* New York: Penguin Putnam, 2000.

Bill Ury is perhaps the most important author writing today on issues of conflict resolution. This book includes practical ways in the home, at work, and around the world to bring peace to our lives.

Cognitive Behavioral Therapy— Managing Fear and Negative Self-Talk

Burns, David D., M.D. *The Feeling Good Handbook.* New York: Penguin Books USA, 1989.

This is an encyclopedic self-help handbook on the cognitive behavioral treatment of depression and anxiety, full of wisdom, direction, and charts galore.

Copeland, Mary Ellen, M.S., and Matthew McKay, Ph.D. *The Depression Workbook: A Guide for Living with Depression and Manic Depression.* Oakland: New Harbinger Publications, 1992.

An excellent, user-friendly guide focused specifically on controlling mood problems.

McKay, Matthew, Ph.D., Martha David, Ph.D., and Patrick Fanning. *Thoughts and Feelings: Taking Control of Your Moods and Your Life.* Oakland: New Harbinger Publications, 1997.

An excellent, user-friendly guide to self-management of depression, anxiety, phobias, anger, and other emotional distress. Good for first-time users of self-help books.

Divorce and Single-Parent Families — Coping for You and Your Children

Benedek, Elissa, M.D., and Catherine Brown. *How to Help Your Child Overcome Your Divorce.* Washington, D.C.: American Psychiatric Press, Inc., 1995.

Dr. Benedek writes with simplicity and gentle wisdom about how to help children of all ages deal with the many feelings resulting from divorce.

Dinkmeyer, Dan, and Gary McKay, and Joyce McKay. *New Beginnings: Skills for Single Parents and Stepfamily Parents, Parent's Manual.* Champaign, Ill.: Research Press, 1987.

Another Research Press winner.

Dolmetsch, Paul, M.S.W., and Alexa Shih, eds. *The Kids' Book about Single-Parent Families.* Garden City, N.Y.: A Dolphin Book, Doubleday & Co., 1985.

This chronology of life in a single-parent family grew out of a writing project the editors oversaw with a group of several dozen students from Burlington, Vermont, most of whom, including the editors, had lived in a single-parent family. You'll love the voices in this book.

Francke, Linda Bird. *Growing Up Divorced.* New York: Linden Press, Simon and Schuster, 1983.

Ms. Francke was an editor at *Newsweek* when she started this project as a cover story that became a book. A number of divorced parents and children in my practice have found this a helpful guide to the pains and stresses of divorce as they emerge at different ages.

McCain, Barbara, M.S.W., and Elissa Benedek, M.D. *What Would You Do? A Child's Book about Divorce.* Illust. James Cummins. Indianapolis: Youth Publications, The Saturday Evening Post, 1976.

This beautifully illustrated book asks young children what they would do if their mom and dad were fighting, yelling, or getting "unmarried."

Mental Disorders — Diagnosis and Resources

American Psychiatric Association. *Diagnostic and Statistical Manual, 4th Edition* (DSM-IV). Washington, D.C.: American Psychiatric Association Press, 1994.

The official diagnostic manual for psychiatry and most of medicine in the United States and around the world. The previous edition, DSM-III-R, was published in 1988.

Barkley, Russell, Ph.D. *Taking Charge of ADHD: The Complete, Authoritative Guide for Parents.* New York: The Guilford Press, 2000.

A world expert on ADHD brings together great information, a little dry in style.

Black, Claudia, M.S.W. *It Will Never Happen to Me!* Denver: M.A.C., 1981.

"If you live in a typical American community, one out of six families in your neighborhood is affected by alcoholism." A helpful guide for people raised in alcoholic families to keep the pain from repeating itself. Over one million copies sold.

Boundy, Dona, M.S.W. *When Money Is the Drug: The Compulsion for Credit, Cash, and Chronic Debt.* San Francisco: HarperCollins Publishers, 1993.

You may need to find this one in a library.

Dean Foundation for Health, Research and Education (books $9, guides $4.50)

Two books and a series of concise, authoritative guides to recognizing and treating specific mental disorders. I give these to my patients. The books and guides are authored by Drs. John Greist and James Jefferson, former senior faculty members in psychiatry at the University of Wisconsin. The books are published by Warner Books, the guides by the Dean Foundation.

> *Anxiety and Its Treatment.* 1986.
>
> *Depression and Its Treatment.* 1992.
>
> *Stimulants and Hyperactive Children: A Guide.* 1990.
>
> *Antipsychotic Medications and Schizophrenia: A Guide.* 1992.
>
> *Panic Disorder and Agoraphobia: A Guide.* 1993.
>
> *Depression and Anti-Depressants: A Guide.* 1995.
>
> *Obsessive Compulsive Disorder: A Guide.* 1995.
>
> *Divalproex and Manic Depression: A Guide.* 1996.
>
> *Fearful Flyers Guide.* 1996.
>
> *Lithium and Manic Depression: A Guide.* 1996.

Hallowell, Edward, M.D., and John Ratey, M.D. *Driven to Distraction: Recognizing and Coping with Attention Deficit Disorder from Childhood through Adulthood.* New York: A Touchstone Book, Simon and Schuster, 1994.

The book many of my distractible patients have read before they seek me out. Makes the transition from childhood to adult attention difficulties.

Jamison, Kay Redfield, Ph.D. *An Unquiet Mind: A Memoir of Moods and Madness.* New York: Vintage Books, Random House, 1995.

Dr. Jamison was on the psychiatric faculty at UCLA when she had her first manic breakdown. She tells a vivid and compelling story of her tortuous journey with mania and depression and what psychiatry has learned about it. She writes in the prologue, "Manic-depression distorts moods and thought, incites dreadful behavior, destroys the basis of rational thought, and too often erodes the desire and will to live. It is an illness that is biological in its origins, yet one that feels psychological in the experience of it; an illness that is unique in conferring advantage and pleasure, yet one that brings in its wake almost unendurable suffering and, not infrequently, suicide." (p. 6)

Koplewicz, Harold S., M.D. *It's Nobody's Fault: New Hope and Help for Difficult Children and Their Parents*. New York: Times Books, Random House, 1996.

A wise and gentle child psychiatrist demystifies "no-fault brain disorders" in childhood and describes their treatments, including attention deficit disorders, obsessive-compulsive disorder, separation anxiety, social phobias/shyness, bedwetting, mood disorders, tics, schizophrenia, eating disorders, conduct disorders, and autism.

Mondimore, Francis Mark, M.D. *Bipolar Disorder: A Guide for Parents and Families*. Baltimore: The Johns Hopkins University Press, 1999.

A friendly, authoritative summary of the history, science, and treatment of mood disorders. Important concluding section titled "Getting Better and Staying Well."

Osborn, Ian, M.D. *Tormenting Thoughts and Secret Rituals: The Hidden Epidemic of Obsessive-Compulsive Disorder*. New York: Pantheon Books, 1998.

Dr. Osborn speaks as a professional who also suffers with OCD. A compassionate, authoritative, readable resource.

Papolos, Demitri, M.D., and Janice Papolos. *The Bipolar Child: The Definitive and Reassuring Guide to Childhood's Most Misunderstood Disorder*. New York: Broadway Books, 1999.

This book is just what it claims to be, definitive and reassuring.

Siegel, Michele, Ph.D., Judith Brisman, Ph.D., and Margot Winshel, M.S.W. *Surviving an Eating Disorder: Strategies for Families and Friends*. New York: Harper and Row, 1988.

An excellent introduction to anorexia nervosa, bulimia, and compulsive overeating and how loved ones can help.

Silver, Larry B., M.D. *The Misunderstood Child: Understanding and Coping with Your Child's Learning Disabilities*. 3d ed. New York: Times Books, Random House, 1998.

When your child's performance in school consistently falls below his or her abilities, you might be dealing with a learning disorder. Here's an expert's guide to sorting through the possible problems and being an advocate for your child.

Styron, William. *Darkness Visible: A Memoir of Madness.* New York: Random House, 1990.

This personal account of agonizing suicidal depression reminds us how depression humbles both sufferers and physicians. The sanctuary of a hospital saved Styron's life despite many trials of early-generation antidepressants. (Medications developed since 1990 are better tolerated and sometimes quicker to work.) An articulate account of the "indescribable" pain of depression and the fact that eventually it lets up.

Wilens, Timothy, M.D. *Straight Talk about Psychiatric Medications for Kids.* New York: The Guilford Press, 1999.

A Harvard child psychiatrist provides parents and practitioners with state-of-the-art information about childhood disorders and the role of medications in their treatment. Helpful for adult patients as well.

Woititz, Janet Geringer, Ed.D. *Struggle for . . . Intimacy.* Pompano Beach, Fla.: Health Communications, Inc., 1985.

Dedicated to adult children of alcoholics, this short book has a wealth of wisdom.

Recovery from Sexual and other Traumas

Bass, Ellen, and Laura Davis. *The Courage to Heal.* New York: Harper and Row, 1988.

Remains one of the best guides to dealing successfully with sexual trauma. Caution! Feelings ignited by this book may seem overwhelming, so take it a little bit at a time. If you get too upset reading it, that's a sign you need to seek help.

Bloom, Sandra. *Creating Sanctuary: Toward the Evolution of Sane Societies.* New York: Routledge, 1997.

Dr. Bloom brings a rich clinical expertise to the creation of healing community for severely traumatized patients and, in doing so, presents a prototype for the larger culture.

Evans, Patricia. *The Verbally Abusive Relationship: How to Recognize It and How to Respond.* 2d ed. Holbrook, Mass: Adams Media Corporation, 1996.

Provides a framework for dealing with abuse of all kinds. If you get too upset reading it, that's a sign you need to seek help.

Hawker, Lynn, Ph.D., and Terry Bicehouse. *End the Pain: Solutions for Stopping Domestic Violence.* New York: Barclay House, 1995.

Two veteran counselors from the Women's Center and Shelter of Greater Pittsburgh share their experience dealing with controllers, abusers, batterers, and their victims. A self-help book with exercises and examples to change abusive relationships.

Herman, Judith Lewis, M.D. *Trauma and Recovery.* New York: Basic Books, 1992.

A rich and readable summary of the effects of trauma on people and ways to heal. It makes a convincing case that political change sometimes must pave the way for emotional and spiritual healing, in this case the women's movement in the 1970s, which propelled child abuse and victimization of women into public awareness.

Terr, Lenore, M.D. *Too Scared to Cry: Psychic Trauma in Childhood.* New York: Basic Books, HarperCollins Publishers, 1990.

Dr. Terr is a master clinician and research child psychiatrist who has treated and studied traumatized children over many years. This sensitive book is packed with compassion and insight into the long-term impacts of childhood trauma.

Wilkomirski, Binjamin. *Fragments: Memories of a Wartime Childhood.* Trans. Carol Brown Janeway. New York: Schocken Books, 1996.

This is a poetic, haunting autobiographical reconstruction of the author's childhood memories of Nazi concentration camps of World War II.

Sexual Orientation and the Family

Clark, Donald H. *Loving Someone Gay.* Berkeley, Calif.: Ten Speed Press, 1997.

The third edition of a classic. Enormous pain often accompanies a person's discovery that he or she is gay or lesbian. This book offers help for the one coming out and for the family.

Dew, Robb Forman. *The Family Heart: A Memoir of When Our Son Came Out.* New York: Ballantine Books, 1995.

A professional writer's poignant autobiography.

Appendix E

COPING WITH A CONTROLLING OR ABUSIVE PARTNER

If you are afraid that your partner will find you reading this book, then you may be caught in an overcontrolling or abusive relationship.

A relationship built on mutual respect guarantees that each party is free to make her or his own choices. In a healthy relationship, partners will not hurt each other intentionally and will make amends when any injury occurs.

If you are in a relationship where you fear for your life or are afraid of the force that will be brought against you, heed your fear. Abusive relationships can lead to severe physical and emotional injuries and sometimes death. The most dangerous time for someone who is routinely controlled and repeatedly mistreated in a relationship is when that person tries to leave. Leaving is the ultimate expression of independence and can bring down the most virulent reprisal.

If you yourself ever become abusive, now is a very good time to stop. You can change. Face your fears of losing control. Creating fear in your partner never makes her or him respect you, much less love you. If you demand that your partner always obey you, get help. You are cheating yourself out of love freely given. You will never know if your partner truly loves you or respects you as long as you are coercing her or him. Maybe love was never freely offered to you. Maybe you like the power and control you feel. Maybe abusing your partner is your way of making sure you are never abandoned or humiliated. Face that fear. You are strong enough. Abusive behavior has no place in any relationship. And it never works forever. If you really want to feel powerful, vanquish your personal ghosts. For help with anger, read *When Anger Hurts: Quieting the Storm Within.*[31]

If you suspect abusive behavior in your family, read Patricia Evans's book *The Verbally Abusive Relationship: How to Recognize It and How to Respond.*[32] She will help you to recognize what's abusive and what's perhaps something else. She defines verbal abuse as "Words that attack or injure, that cause one to believe the false, or that speak falsely of one. Verbal abuse constitutes psychological violence." The key is whether you are free to say no. If you can't say no when that's what you want to say, then there's a real problem in your relationship and it needs to change or you will stay caged in your own fear. Your part may be to confront your own fears of being alone. Many abused people fear that losing their partner means they will never love again. That's a common belief but an unlikely outcome. What's more likely is that you'll find another abusive partner and start the cycle all over again. Or you can get help now and learn the patterns of abusive relationships, how to avoid them, and how to build a healthy new relationship someday.

Staying Can Be Dangerous—So Can Leaving

The average battered spouse tries more than five times to leave before actually escaping the abusive situation. Then if the batterer finds the spouse, the abused spouse faces the highest risk of being assaulted again, stalked, or murdered.

In large measure thanks to the 1970s women's movement and its campaign of public awareness about abuse, many communities today have shelter organizations that can hide terrorized women and their children and provide financial, emotional, and spiritual support in times of danger. Seek advice about how to protect yourself and your children. Create a plan and carry it out. Services for battered men are more difficult to find because their numbers are fewer and public awareness of the problem is more recent. Nonetheless, contact your local service agencies and see what help they can offer.

- Look in the community services pages under "Abuse/Assault" in the front of your local telephone book.
- Call your local crisis clinic and ask for help in planning your escape.

- Meet privately with someone who can help you create your plan.
- If all else fails, call 911 or your local police and ask them for help.

Domestic violence ordinances, which afford some measure of protection, have taken root throughout the United States in the past several decades. In Seattle you can call the local police if you are being assaulted or repeatedly threatened with assault and two officers will come to your home. If an assault occurred, the offending party will be automatically taken to jail. If no assault occurred this time, the police will inform your partner that any assault will result in jail time and that you have grounds for filing an antiharassment petition. You also have the option to leave with the police officers to avoid retaliation when they leave and to allow a cooling-off period. If you fear going home to retaliation afterward, then you should find a safe place to go instead.

For battered women shelters, call the national hotline for the 800 number in your area: 800-799-SAFE (800-799-7233). For information about organizations that support abused and battered women, call 800-537-2238.

Appendix F

MORE ABOUT MENTAL DISORDERS AND HOW TO FIND HELP

Mental disorders do not usually take away our entire capacity to do useful work, care for our families, or continue to enjoy life. Rather, mental disorders impose obstacles that make whatever we do more difficult. By definition, the quality of our work, our life outside of work, or our health must suffer before difficulties can be diagnosed as a mental disorder. We become more easily overwhelmed in the presence of a mental disorder than we would if we did not have the disorder. The more severe the disruptions, the higher the likelihood we will become disabled by them.

Duration of difficulty and severity of disability distinguish ongoing mental disorders from transient problems in life. What are merely bumps in the road as opposed to mountainous terrain that defines the rest of our lives? The difference lies in how quickly and completely we can bounce back from adversity and how readily we adapt to circumstances beyond our control. Mental disorders tend to become chronic and to undermine our abilities to fight back effectively, whereas life crises resolve in the course of healthy struggle.

Mental disorders make our lives more difficult the way raising the incline on a treadmill makes walking more difficult. We become exhausted more easily and have to work harder to go the distance we used to be able to accomplish when the terrain was flatter. If we do not notice the steeper slope, we may expect ourselves to perform as if no change has occurred. The steeper the slope, the closer we get to our coping and endurance limits and the more frustration and self-criticism await us.

Many people fear the stigma of mental illness almost as much as they fear mental illness itself. Such fear and stigma are widespread, understandable, and misplaced. Bias against mental illness is like racial and ethnic prejudice and burdens millions of lives in a similar way. However, the stigma of admitting you need help will surely be more bearable than suffering the continuous burden of unrecognized or untreated mental illness.

Encephalitis is clearly an infection of the brain with known consequences regarding the way people function—sometimes causing loss of intellectual capacity or more specific functions such as hearing, sight, or the ability to socialize comfortably. This is acknowledged to be a medical illness of the brain. A brain tumor is likewise defined as a medical illness. With delirium—a brain-based state of confusion caused by fever, metabolic imbalances, or toxic compounds in the body—the boundary between medical and mental illness gets blurred, which is good. Mental illnesses are medical illnesses. The one area of confusion is behavioral disorders generated and sustained by external reinforcement, but even some of these have a clearly biological component that helps explain the disability.

When people are severely depressed, they may know they need to exercise, speak supportively and patiently with their children, get enough sleep, and eat well, but they simply cannot do it for lack of energy and will. Being clinically depressed is like swimming in a vat of molasses while convinced there is no way out. It's a biological implosion of our mental capacity to think clearly. Addiction to alcohol similarly saps our motivation and capacity to care about the people we love. High anxiety makes our molehill worries seem impossible to overcome.

Unrecognized mental disorders can make a sane family feel crazy. Families seeking to heal from chronic conflict need to learn as quickly as possible if any mental disorders are compounding their problems. Someone who is depressed, excessively anxious, persistently distractible, addicted, obsessive, learning disabled, or delusional will have a much harder time cooperating in a recovery process. Most of these problems respond dramatically to appropriate help, including education about the illness, special coping strategies that include behavioral management and psychotherapy, and targeted medications.

If you find disabling, persistent symptoms in members of your immediate family, whether or not you find a description of those symptoms in appendix B, an early psychiatric evaluation could save your family mountains of ongoing frustration. Family physicians are getting better at diagnosing straightforward mental illnesses. Your best bet, however, will be with a psychiatrist (M.D. or D.O.) because psychiatrists are experts in diagnosing mental disorders and they can prescribe medicines appropriate to biological mental disorders.

To find a psychiatrist, try the following:

- Ask your family doctor for a referral.
- Call your health insurance carrier for a referral.
- Check with friends to see if any of them have found good help.
- Call your state psychiatric association.
- Call the American Psychiatric Association in Washington, D.C. (888-357-7924) and ask for a local referral.
- For help with your children and adolescents, call the American Academy of Child and Adolescent Psychiatry, also in Washington, D.C. (202-966-7300) for a local referral.

Insurance coverage may not be what you think or hope it is, so be sure to check with your insurance company about coverage for the individual psychiatrist you want to see. Otherwise, you will end up paying the costs out of your own pocket. You can also choose to pay privately if you want to work with a specific doctor who is not covered by your insurance or you don't want confidential information entered into computerized insurance records.

Mental Illness Can Be Inherited

Many of these powerfully disruptive biological mental disorders are transmitted in the family genes. If we consider the possibility that our parents' shortcomings were based in part in undiagnosed biological mental disorders, then perhaps we can forgive them more easily and get on with making helpful choices now.

Mona's boyfriend got so drunk and obnoxious at their college graduation party that she burst into tears of fury and embarrassment as soon as she tried to tell me about it. She quickly focused on her father, who had regularly spoiled family gatherings and her teenage parties with friends. Somehow the idea that both these men were addicted to alcohol rather than unloving or malicious people helped her to accept her losses and to focus more clearly on dating men who had their addictive tendencies under better control.

As we replace blaming others for their misdeeds with an understanding that they never learned to cope with mental illness, we begin to move beyond our hurt and anger to confronting the emotional injuries we still carry. This is an important developmental milestone. We are now free to use our energy in more creative ways. Understanding our parents' frailty helps us with our own children's hurt and anger.

What Is Illness and What Is Me?

How clearly are the symptoms of mental disorders different from the traits we define as parts of ourselves? People diagnosed with mental disorders routinely struggle to separate self from illness. Someone who is hypomanic may well enjoy feeling expansive, friendly, and flirtatious until the episode ends in a precipitous drop into depression. The symptoms of hypomania are unhealthy exaggerations of otherwise desirable attributes, and they are largely beyond the individual's voluntary control. As such, they significantly limit a person's real choices to be energetic and productive, but the high energy and creativity of the highs can be very pleasurable, especially early in the course of the illness. Separating an illness like this from one's innate self is a complex and difficult task that benefits from regular feedback from caring people and often from psychotherapy as well.

Healthy individuals find ways to adapt to their biological legacies and integrate them into ways of feeling unique and competent in the world. You needn't worry about a mental disorder unless you have persistent and disruptive problems in your ability to get along with the people close to you. If these difficulties fail to improve with corrective efforts, then the possibility of a mental disorder increases.

In families with chronic fighting, the odds may be very high that someone has a treatable mental disorder, that is, a mental disorder with a clear biological component that would benefit from appropriate treatment. Such treatment starts with a comprehensive psychiatric evaluation that includes a careful history of individual and family problems, physical and emotional symptoms, and current functioning. Choices for treatment are then tailored to the individual and could include medicine, psychotherapy, guided self-help, or referral for more specialized help.

If you suspect mental illness in your family, review your family's history. Sketch your family tree, showing who is biologically related to whom. Besides your parents, include grandparents on both sides of your family, as well as your aunts and uncles and all their offspring. Fill in as much information as you have on each individual regarding symptoms or diagnoses of physical and mental illness. Include physical illnesses such as cancer, diabetes, heart disease, and high blood pressure, and include a cause of death for those who have died. This information helps you understand the stresses that may run in your family. Include traumatic events where someone's life was in danger—a fire, combat warfare, rape, witnessing an assault. Include alcohol use, drug use, depression, anxiety, mood swings, obsessions, distractibility, chronic irritability, psychosis, and suicide. List any treatments or hospital visits you know about. If you can, ask others in your family who might have additional information.[33] Family secrets may be hard to ferret out but can be important clues to current troubles and possible solutions. This family history will be very helpful in finding patterns of inherited difficulty in your family.

The bottom line is that you do yourself a favor to identify and find effective treatment for any mental disorder in your family.

Appendix G

PARENT SKILLS TRAINING

My favorite resource for basic parent skills is Gerald R. Patterson's *Families: Applications of Social Learning to Family Life*. Dr. Patterson presents the collective wisdom acquired through the Oregon Research Institute, a program that worked with difficult and delinquent children and youth and developed a refined strategy for parents based on social learning experiments. "This book is written for parents and for other people who need to know how families 'work.'"[33] It is especially helpful for dealing with challenging children. His chapter titled "Accidental Training: Unplanned Reinforcement" sold me on this approach. "It is a paradox that sometimes we create reinforcement arrangements that train our close friends, members of our families, and others whom we love to display high rates of problem behaviors. We also set up reinforcements that strengthen problem behavior in ourselves. Such programs are extremely effective, even though they are unplanned." (p. 25) Although written in 1975, *Families* is still the best short book about parenting I have found. It is available through major booksellers.

Learn about Normal Child Development and Build Your Skills

Fortunately for parents, there is now an abundance of excellent parenting books, all building on the early work of authors like Dr. Patterson. Start with learning about how healthy children grow and change, sometimes month by month. Frances Ilg and Louise Ames set the standard thirty years ago with *Childhood Behavior* and authored a revised book in 1996. Ann Vernon and Radhi Al-Mabuk have another useful guide (cited below). Several newer books on building your parenting skills are cited in the text and in appendix D. You will do yourself a real favor to read several of these and buy one or two as reference books for ongoing study.

I have come to trust several publishers for reliable, authoritative self-help books. Research Press of Champaign, Illinois, provides excellent books for parents and educators on many topics of child and family emotional health. Here are three of them:

- Vernon, Ann, Ph.D., and Radhi Al-Mabuk, Ph.D. *What Growing Up Is All About: A Parent's Guide to Child and Adolescent Development.* 1995.

  Drs. Vernon and Al-Mabuk are professors at Northern Iowa University. They write, "By understanding more about [normal child and adolescent] developmental stages, parents have a 'road map' to refer to in determining whether children or adolescents are reaching their destinations or if they have detoured and need extra support and intervention." (p. viii) Some of the section titles in the book include "Effective Parenting," "Communication and Discipline," "The Preschool Years," "Middle Childhood," "Early Adolescence," "Mid-Adolescence," and "When the Problems Don't Seem So Normal."

- Blechman, Elaine A., Ph.D. *Solving Child Behavior Problems at Home and at School.* 1985.

  Dr. Blechman, a professor at Albert Einstein College of Medicine in the Bronx, New York, specializes in behavioral family therapy. Her approach targets both children's problem behaviors and enhancing parental competence in and out of the home. Included in the book are problem-solving modules designed for therapists, parents, and teachers, covering issues such as bedtime, toileting, temper tantrums, school attendance, allowances, homework, television, loneliness, and self-injury.

- Silberman, Mel, Ph.D. *When Your Child Is Difficult: Solve Your Toughest Child-Raising Problems with a Four-Step Plan That Works.* 1995.

  Dr. Silberman, a professor of psychological studies in education at Temple University, writes, "This book has one overriding goal: to give parents (and all other child-care providers) the confidence to help children change their behavior when they are being difficult." He outlines the Four-Step Plan: Get clear what you want, remain calm and confident, select a plan of action, and obtain support from other adults. Distinguished Professor Arnold Lazarus says of this book, "One of the best parenting books you'll ever read."

Other books I have found helpful include the following:

- Borcherdt, Bill. *Making Families Work and What to Do When They Don't: Thirty Guides for Imperfect Parents of Imperfect Children.* New York: The Haworth Press, 1996.
- Dinkmeyer, Don, Gary McKay, and Joyce McKay. *New Beginnings: Skills for Single Parents and Stepfamily Parents, Parents' Manual.* Champaign, Ill.: Research Press, 1987.
- Dolmetsch, Paul, and Alexa Shih, eds. *The Kids' Book about Single-Parent Families.* Garden City, N.Y.: A Dolphin Book, Doubleday & Co., 1985.
- Napier, Augustus, and Carl Whitaker. *The Family Crucible: One Family's Therapy—An Experience That Illuminates All Our Lives.* New York: Bantam Books, 1978.
- Scott, Virginia, George Doub, and Peggy Runnels. *Raising a Loving Family.* Holbrook, Mass.: Adams Media Corporation, 1999.

Endnotes

1. P. C. Glick, "The Role of Divorce in the Changing Family Structure: Trends and Variations, in *Children of Divorce: Empirical Perspectives on Adjustment,* ed. S. A. Wolchik and P. Karoly (eds.), New York: Gardner, 1988, 3–34; Kenneth Kendler et al., Survey responses were evaluated using the DSM III-R, the American medical community's official manual for diagnosis of mental and behavioral disorders as of 1990, *Archives of General Psychiatry* 51 (1994): 8–19; "Current Trends in Child Abuse Prevention, Reporting, and Fatalities: The 1999 Fifty State Survey, National Center on Child Abuse Prevention Research, 200 S. Michigan Ave., Chicago, IL 60604, p. 13; National Institute of Mental Health, "Suicide Facts," http://www.nimh.nif.gov/research/suifact.htm.

2. Portia Nelson, *There's a Hole in My Sidewalk: The Romance of Self-Discovery* (Hillsboro, Ore.: Beyond Words Publishing, 1994), pp. 2–3.

3. Stephen Glenn, Ph.D., and Jane Nelson, Ed.D., *Raising Self-Reliant Children in a Self-Indulgent World: Seven Building Blocks for Developing Capable Young People,* rev. ed. (Roseville, Calif.: Prima Publishing, 2000), p. 9.

4. John Nichols and Robert McChesney, *It's the Media, Stupid* (New York: Seven Stories Press, 2000), pp. 28, 33.

5. Mary Pipher, Ph.D., *The Shelter of Each Other: Rebuilding Our Families* (New York: Ballantine Books, 1997), p. 9.

6. Patricia Owen, "For Models and Centerfolds, Thin Is Dangerously In" (unpublished study, St. Mary's University, 1998).

7. If your child has difficulties getting along with other children, try reading together with your child *Good Friends Are Hard to Find: Help Your Child Find, Make and Keep Friends* (Los Angeles: Perspective Publishing, 1996) by Fred Frankel, Ph.D. This is a child-friendly book about making

friends and dealing with teasing, bullying, and other difficult childhood social situations.

8. Kenneth Kendler et al. *Archives of General Psychiatry* vol. 51 (1994), pp. 8–19. Survey responses were evaluated using the *DSM-III-R*, the American medical community's official manual for diagnosis of mental and behavioral disorders at the time. The next and current edition, *DSM-IV*, was published in 1994.

9. Statistics reported by the National Institute on Alcohol Abuse and Alcoholism, National Institutes of Health, 1995 (http://silk.nih.gov/silk/niaaa/database/abdep4.txt).

10. Appendix B presents a short list based on the *Diagnostic and Statistical Manual of Mental Disorders,* 1994 edition (*DSM-IV*), American Psychiatric Association. The *DSM-IV* is the official diagnostic code for American psychiatry and is now generally accepted throughout the medical field in many parts of the world.

11. The reasons for this gender difference are not clear. Some researchers suggest that reproductive hormones play a role. One researcher found in one sample of inpatient psychiatric admissions that the increased incidence of sexual abuse among women may account for it (Nicholas Ward, M.D., personal communication, *1997*).

12. Harville and Helen Hendrix have written several popular books about family legacies and their impact on our parenting, including *Getting the Love You Want* and *Giving the Love That Heals.* (See appendix D for the references.)

13. Now available under the title *Banner in the Sky* by James Ramsey Ullman (New York: HarperCollins Publishers, 1988).

14. The Convention on the Rights of the Child was adopted by the United Nations General Assembly on 20 November 1989 and entered into force on 2 September 1990. As of publication, the United States is the only nation that still has not signed.

15. Excerpt from the preamble to the Convention on the Rights of the Child.

16. Variations on the Golden Rule can be found in the teachings of Christianity, Judaism, Confucianism, Sikhism, Buddhism, Hinduism, Zoroastrianism, and others.

17. Dick Gregory, *Nigger, An Autobiography*, with Robert Lipsyte (New York: Washington Square Press, 1964), pp. 40–41.

18. Ibid, p. 132.

19. George R. Bach and Peter Wyden, *The Intimate Enemy: How to Fight Fair in Love and Marriage* (New York: William Morrow and Co., 1969).

20. R. A. Spitz, "Hospitalis: An Inquiry into the Genesis of Psychiatric Conditions of Early Childhood," *Psychoanalytic Study of the Child* 1 (1945): 53–74.

21. For more help with storytelling, see Doris Brett, *Annie Stories* (New York: Workman Publishing, 1988). Brett shares how she created stories to help her daughter with fears, a new baby, school, divorce, going to the hospital, and more.

22. Terry Orlick, *The Cooperative Sports & Games Book: Challenge without Competition* (New York: Pantheon Books, 1978).

23. Alice Miller, *For Your Own Good: Hidden Cruelty in Child-Rearing and the Roots of Violence* (New York: Farrar Straus Giroux, 1983), p. xviv.

24. Thomas Harris, *I'm OK, You're OK: The Transactional Analysis Breakthrough That's Changing the Consciousness and Behavior of People Who Never Before Felt OK about Themselves* (New York: Avon Books/HarperCollins Publishers, 1973), pp. 72–73.

25. See Ricky Greenwald, Psy.D. *Trauma and Juvenile Delinquency: Theory, Research, and Interventions* (forthcoming).

26. The American Association of University Women published a report in 1991 titled *Shortchanging Girls, Shortchanging America* in which they found girls markedly less self-confident than boys on a variety of measures including feeling happy and future careers. See also Peggy Orenstein, *Schoolgirls: Young Women, Self-Esteem, and the Confidence Gap* (New York: Anchor Books, 1994).

27. See appendix C for contact information.

28. Erikson, Erik H., *Childhood and Society*, 2d ed. (New York: W.W. Norton and Co., 1963), p. 267.

29. William Ury, *Getting Past No*, rev. ed. (New York: Bantam Books, 1993), pp. 31–156.

30. Descriptions of each of these nine disorders are based on diagnostic criteria from the *Diagnostic and Statistical Manual)*, 4th Ed. (Washington, D.C.: American Psychiatric Association Press, 1994).

31. McKay, Matthew, Ph.D., Peter D. Rogers, Ph.D., and Judith McKay, R.N., *When Anger Hurts: Quieting the Storm Within* (Oakland: New Harbinger Publications, 1989).

32. Patricia Evans, *The Verbally Abusive Relationship: How to Recognize It and How to Respond*, exp. 2d ed. (Holbrook, Mass.: Adams Media Corporation, 1996).

33. Elizabeth Carter and Monica McGoldrick describe how to create a family genogram in their book, *The Family Lifecycle: A Framework for Family Therapy* (New York: Gardner Press, Inc., 1980), p. xxiii.

34. Gerald Patterson, *Families* (Champaign, Ill.: Research Press, 1975), p. 1.

INDEX

ABOUT THE AUTHOR

David C. Hall, M.D., is a child and adolescent psychiatrist and a third-generation physician. He has been helping hundreds of families in the Seattle, Washington, area since 1983. From children as young as two to grandparents as old as eighty-nine, his patients have found kind and expert guidance for a wide range of seemingly hopeless problems.

Born in Seattle, Dr. Hall graduated from Harvard College and the University of Washington School of Medicine. He finished his psychiatric training in 1983 with an award for clinical excellence. In 1986 he completed a year's study with the Montlake Family Therapy Institute. He is a member of the American Academy of Child and Adolescent Psychiatry, the American Psychiatric Association, and the American Society for Clinical Psychopharmacology.

While working intensively with individual families in his private practice, Dr. Hall has volunteered thousands of hours in grass-roots programs dedicated to preserving a healthy local and global environment for children and families. He is a founding steering committee member of the Child Violence Identification and Prevention Project and a board member of the Black Dollar Days Task Force, an inner-city microlending program. In 1997 he served as national president of Physicians for Social Responsibility, the U.S. affiliate of International Physicians for the Prevention of Nuclear War, which in 1985 received the Nobel Peace Prize.

Dr. Hall is also an active member of University Baptist Church in Seattle, where his wife of more than thirty years, the Reverend Anne Hall, is a co-pastor. They have two grown sons and recently became grandparents for the first time.

LECTURES, SEMINARS, AND SERVICES AVAILABLE

Dr. Hall offers a variety of speeches, talks, and seminars. His talks can be geared toward parents and grandparents, professionals who work with children and troubled families, or any community or religious group interested in promoting healthier and happier families.

Call or write today for full information on booking Dr. Hall to speak at your next meeting or conference. Dr. Hall will carefully customize his talk for you and your group's needs.

For further information about Dr. Hall's activities, seminar schedule, consulting services or programs, contact Dr. Hall at

Montlake Family Press
2200 - 24th Avenue East
Seattle, Washington 98112
(888) 565-3404
www.FamilyHealing.com